F   er

		DATE DUE	

Cover photo: National Archives of Canada,
accession 1987-071, frame # CC-94-2-9

Canadian Cataloguing in Publication Data

Penner, Norman, 1921-
     From protest to power.

Includes index.
ISBN 1-55028-385-5 (bound). ISBN 1-55028-384-7 (pbk.)

1. Socialism - Canada - History. 2. Social reformers - Canada. 3. Canada - Politics and government - 20th century. 4. Co-operative Commonwealth federation. 5. New Democratic Party.
HX109.P45 1992   320.5'31'097109   C92-093759-4

James Lorimer & Company, Publishers
Egerton Ryerson Memorial Building
35 Britain Street
Toronto, Ontario
M5A 1R7   " 33853

Printed in Canada

Acknowledgements

I extend my appreciation to the Social Sciences and Humanities Research Council of Canada (SSHRC) for the generous grant, without which it would have been impossible to finish the book.

I thank Professor Paul Lovejoy, then Vice-President in charge of Research at York University, for his encouragement and help in the preparation of my application for the grant.

I was able to secure research assistants of the highest calibre—Ken Rivkin, Vancouver; Elaine Frank, Edmonton; Maureen Lux, Saskatoon and Regina; Jean-Marc Hebert, Winnipeg; Malcolm Davidson, Ottawa. I acknowledge heartily the contribution they have made to my book.

I owe much to Noli Swatman, Lori Rossi, and Samuel Sui, who administered the grant with efficiency and courtesy.

And finally, my thanks to Norma Penner, who assisted me greatly in preparing the manuscript for the publisher, and to John Boyd for his expert editing, which I have come to rely on, with confidence.

Contents

Preface

This study, *From Protest to Power*, concentrates on the growth in Canada of social democracy in ideological and political terms, from the beginning of this century to the present, tracing its various forms, its heritage, and its most important expression as the third party in Canadian politics.

Through various twists and turns, the social democratic movement founded a national political party, the Co-operative Commonwealth Federation (CCF), and later on the New Democratic Party (NDP). The NDP has a new status: it has become, for the first time, the government in Ontario, has again formed the governments in British Columbia and Saskatchewan, is the official opposition in Manitoba, and now holds forty-four seats, a record for the party, in the House of Commons.

Social democracy began to develop as an independent force in the labour and farmers' movement at the turn of the century, but it was not until 1933 that this amorphous grouping came together to form a political party. It first appeared as protest movements in the trade unions, farmers' associations, women's groups, youth movements, and eventually appeared as the program of independent groups that came forward as third parties in municipal, provincial and federal elections. Social democracy continues to be expressed through various mass movements, but since 1933 it has been expressed more powerfully through a federal-provincial parliamentary party.

Mass movements change from period to period, in their character and in the nature of the demands they put forward. They often start spontaneously, gathering supporters from all parties, but in practice, they have made their most significant impact on the NDP.

But social democracy as it appeared at the beginning of this century included the socialist idea, a doctrine which appealed to growing sections of the working class and middle-class intellectuals, and which challenged the dominant liberalism and reformism of that period. Above all, the socialism of western Europe and Britain had already garnered millions of voters in those countries. In Canada, most of the social democratic parties made the idea of socialism, whether Marxist or Fabian, the central distinguishing feature of their political program. But why did it take so long before a social democratic parliamentary party, national in scope, was established in Canada, as contrasted with Great Britain, Europe, Australia, and New Zealand, which had flourishing parties long before? This is a major theme of this book.

By the time the Co-operative Commonwealth Federation was launched, the world struggle between capitalism and socialism had also become the struggle between socialism and communism, and this placed additional obstacles in the path of a fledgling social democratic party trying to get off the ground. As far as the communists in Canada were concerned, their fight against capitalism included the fight against social democracy, which often took precedence over capitalism as their main enemy.

The opponents of the NDP, who have always equated social democracy with communism, have now stepped up their propaganda by suggesting that the fall of communism is at the same time the fall of social democracy. There are members and followers of the NDP today who urge the party to adopt a new program, which would eliminate or downplay socialism, and constitute a turn to the right. Some of the advocates of this approach were formerly critics from the left, attacking the NDP for not being socialist enough. J. S. Woodsworth consistently fought for his definition of socialism from 1918 on. It may be, as some have suggested, that it was his insistence on having a socialist program that slowed down the foundation of the CCF until 1933. But that is now a matter of speculation. Most of the delegates who attended the founding convention came together to found a party that openly stated its socialist aims. There were some who thought that the program should have a more Marxist flavour, but at the end, Woodsworth's approach, contained in the Regina Manifesto, and in his President's Address, was adopted.

His definition was brief, but meaningful. It was an application of Fabianism to Canadian conditions. It was a program which distinguished the CCF not only from communism, but — more important in the Canadian setting — from Liberal reformism. It was not only Woodsworth versus Marx, but Woodsworth versus Mackenzie King.

And because of the year in which the party was founded, it was also a program to fight the ravages of the Great Depression.

Because of this, it became obvious later that many proposals in the Regina Manifesto were outdated, and had to be replaced. This was done periodically, and often aroused sharp debates, basically centering on the definition or description of the party's understanding of socialism.

The major changes along these lines took place at the Winnipeg CCF convention of 1956, the change from CCF to NDP in 1961, and at the party's fiftieth anniversary convention in 1983. The main assault on the principles of the party from within its ranks came from the movement around the Waffle Manifesto, which wanted a much greater emphasis on socialism. A new debate, just beginning, aims to recast the basic foundations of Canadian social democracy, and either leave out socialism entirely, or merge socialism with capitalism, giving full freedom to the market economy.

Socialism in various forms — social democracy, democratic socialism, revolutionary or "scientific" socialism — has been debated for well over a century. The Soviet or Marxist-Leninist model, which was supposedly based on Karl Marx's revolutionary idea of the "dictatorship of the proletariat," has collapsed. But there have been, and still are, governments, led by social-democratic parties, which admit that while their societies are not yet socialist, they have socialism as their goal.

Canadian social democracy has developed along a slower road to power than has been the experience in most other countries that have social democratic parties. Yet, with all its shortcomings, it now has more support and status than ever before. It also has become more moderate. In spite of this, however, the opposition to it is more hysterical, more venomous, and more heavily financed.

But the proponents of social democracy continue to travel along the road which they believe will lead to socialism, however that road is ultimately defined. But on that road, they will be the main force to initiate and defend reforms for the people, and to use their political power to that end.

To my grandchildren:
Dylan, Emma, and Jacob

1

Liberalism and Socialism in the Nineteenth Century

Although Canada came into existence with the proclamation of the British North America Act, July 1, 1867, it was still a colony of Great Britain and remained so, juridically at least, until the Statute of Westminster, 1931. But it provided the emerging Canadian capitalists, mainly centred in Montreal and Toronto, a half continent over which they could establish and dominate their market. By the end of the century, Canada stretched from "sea unto sea," and had a transcontinental railway, a canal system astride the St. Lawrence River, a flourishing ocean port at Halifax, the opening of the soil-rich western prairies — all buttressed by the financial outpouring of British investors, then the richest in the world.

Canada now needed urgently hundreds of thousands of immigrants to supply the labour force for the factories and the farms. They came, with government assistance, from Britain, the United States, and Central and Eastern Europe.

Many of them came with political and social outlooks that had already developed or were developing in their homelands. Some brought deeply embedded religious views; others brought more recently developed ideas—socialist, social-democratic, and trade union.

It may seem arbitrary to say that socialist and trade union ideas began to take root in Canada at the turn of the century. But this was largely so, especially because of the industrial revolution that changed the face of Britain, and the preponderance of British workers who came to Canada in the period from 1900 to 1914. Most Canadian historians have neglected to make this analysis, but it is vital to an

understanding of how and why the Canadian social democratic movement began to develop at this time.

Liberalism and socialism were the main theoretical outgrowths of
the commercial and industrial revolutions which ushered in modern
bourgeois society. Liberalism as the ideological expression of the
bourgeois interest came first, and had implanted its theories well
before the industrial revolution produced an industrial proletariat and
a body of thought that sought to express its aims and concerns. Trade
unionism generally preceded socialism, but by the end of the
nineteenth century, working-class parties had emerged which brought
together both trade unions and socialist parties. In continental Europe,
most of these parties looked to the doctrine of Karl Marx as their
theoretical guide, whereas in Britain the Labour Party, founded in
1906, rejected the idea of adopting a single doctrine, allowing several
doctrines to coexist within a loosely organized federated party. However, after the Chartist movements had fought for most of the
nineteenth century for democratic reforms, the Labour Party was
wedded firmly to the parliamentary system.

The idea that society works best in a system of representative
government was one of the major new ideas of the liberal bourgeoisie,
particularly in Britain, but John Locke, one of the earliest protagonists
of liberalism, insisted that only those who had property should be
allowed to participate. However, it took almost 150 years after Locke
before the middle class was given the vote, and forty years after that
before most of the property qualifications were removed, thus allowing most men over the age of 21 to vote and stand as candidates.

Writing at a time when the middle class was fighting for the right
to vote, Jeremy Bentham, a prominent liberal philosopher, saw an
identity of interest between what he called the "productive classes,"
namely the manufacturers and the workers, and a conflict between
them and the "non-productive" classes, the aristocracy and the monar-
chy. He denied that universal manhood suffrage would be subversive
to the rights of property.

Bentham believed, as did his colleague, James Mill, that one of the
principal reasons for advocating manhood suffrage was to win the
support of the masses in the struggle against the aristocracy, which
at that time had control of the political system.

James Mill, in his *Essay on Government* said:

> There can be no doubt that the middle rank which gives
> to science, to art, and to legislation itself, their most dis-

tinguished ornaments, and is the chief source of all that has exalted and refined human nature, is that portion of the community of which, if the basis of representation were ever so extended, the opinion would ultimately decide. Of the people beneath them a vast majority would be sure to be guided by their advice and example. [1]

But it was also clear that no reforms in the electoral system, or for that matter in factory legislation, which Bentham and Mill advocated could supersede or in any way undermine the property rights of the middle classes:

When security (of property) and equality are in opposition there should be no hesitation: equality should give way ... The establishment of equality is a chimera: the only thing which can be done is to diminish inequality. [2]

Indeed, the "radical reformers," or "philosophic radicals" as they were called, did have an influence on the working class for the first part of the century. Their advocacy of parliamentary and electoral reform, their support of social measures to ameliorate the widespread suffering of the poor and to relieve the terrible conditions in the factories, held out hope that an enlightened middle class could be effective in bringing substantial improvement to the daily lives of the working class. But as the workers, or at least sections of them, became more militant and class conscious, they developed distinctive ideas which went beyond the ideology of the middle class. They did not share the view of Bentham that the manufacturers were part of the productive classes. From the ideas of John Locke and the political economists, such as Adam Smith and David Ricardo, who said that labour is the creator of all wealth, they concluded that labour is entitled to a much greater share than mere subsistence.

Robert Owen, a manufacturer who was one of the earliest exponents of what he called in 1813 "A New View of Society," became associated with the first trade unions, with the co-operative movement, and later with the propagation of socialist ideas. Frederick Engels, co-worker of Karl Marx, called Owen the founder of English socialism.[3] Owen at first adopted the utilitarian philosophy of Bentham and others,

> ...that man is born with a desire to obtain happiness,
> which desire is the primary cause of all his actions, con-
> tinues through life, and in popular language is called "self
> interest."[4]

But Owen went beyond the individualism of the utilitarians, pro-
posing the community or collective interest as the only arbiter by
which the masses of people could advance:

> That principle is the happiness of self, clearly understood
> and uniformly practised; which can only be attained by
> conduct that must promote the happiness of the commu-
> nity.[5]

Owen wrote extensively about the conditions of the working class,
or what he called the "lower orders," which he described with great
indignation. He condemned child labour, subsistence wages, abject
poverty, the iniquitous poor laws, the absence of public education,
and the dreadful slums. He declared that the people had the right to
work, and that the government was obligated to take up the slack
during depressions, "to provide perpetual employment of real national
utility, in which all who apply may be immediately occupied."[6]

In these early writings Owen addressed himself mainly to his
fellow manufacturers, because he believed then that they would act
in a rational and social manner if they could be shown that it would
be to their benefit. He even set up a model community to demonstrate
his theory.

He also addressed himself to the working class, believing that they
would understand the justice of his appeal:

> While you show by your conduct any desire violently to
> dispossess the manufacturers — is it not evident that they
> must regard you with jealous and hostile feelings, that the
> contention between rich and poor will never have an end
> and that whatever relative changes take place among you,
> there will ever be the same oppression of the weak and the
> party who has attained to power? Before your condition
> can be ameliorated this useless contest must cease, and
> measures must be adopted in which both parties may have
> a substantial interest.[7]

Although Owen became frustrated and impatient over the lack of a response to his appeals and to the model community, his appeals for moderation became one of the characteristic features of the British labour and socialist movement.

Frederick Engels wrote in 1858 about England having a "bourgeois proletariat," while Owen was becoming more radical.[8] Owen never raised the question of the transfer of power by the working class, nor did he attack the capitalist right to acquire and extend ownership of property. Nor did he challenge the right of the capitalist to buy and exploit the labour of others. He rejected the idea that man was inherently individualistic, claiming that man's innate nature changes as the surrounding society changes, and can turn from a society based on competition to one based on co-operation.[9]

Marx later took up this idea in his *Theses on Ludwig Fuerbach*, giving credit to Owen for originating this thesis:

> The materialist doctrine that men are products of circumstances and upbringing and that, therefore, changed men are products of other circumstances and changed upbringing, forgets that circumstances are changed precisely by men and that the educator must himself be educated. Hence this doctrine necessarily arrives at dividing society into two parts, one towers above society (in Robert Owen, for example).
>
> The coincidence of the changing circumstances can only be conceived and rationally understood as revolutionary practice.[10]

Robert Owen made another important contribution to socialist thought by expanding on the labour theory of value, which had been accepted by British political economists as essential to the phenomenon of exchange. Owen used the theory to justify an increased share for the workers from the capital which they produce.

Although Owen did not go beyond the idea that the worker should be paid "a fair and fixed proportion of all the wealth he creates,"[11] some of his contemporaries and followers, using the same arguments, attacked the property holders, and denied that they had any right to a share in the wealth which the workers produced.

John Gray was one of the first to establish a clear distinction between radicalism and socialism:

The persons who furnish the subject of our present consideration, are living upon property which is not naturally
their own. They are living upon property of which the
productive classes are the true proprietors, and of which
they have been deprived by the force of circumstances.
The property they live upon is not theirs: they did not
create it: they have given no equivalent for it. We defy
them to show by any principle of justice, that they have
any right whatever to it.[12]

The foundation of all property is Labour. There is no
other just foundation for it…in fact all property is nothing
more than accumulated labour.[13]

The land itself is of no value until labour be applied to
it. It is its produce only that is valuable. What does the
landlord do towards the production of it? He does nothing!
Then we say that no part of it whatever can be his. It was
exclusively produced by the labour of others…it is exclusively their property.[14]

The significance of Gray's argument is that he took Locke's natural right — the right of an individual to the product of his labour —
and made it a class right by excluding the right to private appropria-
tion of another man's labour which Locke had added to it.

When the first political party based upon the working class was
formed in Britain in 1831, its manifesto carried the slogan "Labour
Is the Source of All Wealth." For the working class to make an impact
politically, it needed such an estimation of its own worth and of its
importance to the nation.

The Chartist movement was not strictly socialist, although many
of its members and followers were. But it certainly recognized itself
as a working-class movement, fighting for the political rights of this
class. According to the official statistics, there were 6,023,752 males
twenty-one years and over who were denied the vote, as compared
with 839,519 who, because of the property they owned, were the only
ones entitled to elect or be elected.

The movement was plagued with internal divisions between those
who argued for change through peaceful agitation and those who felt
that the peaceful means had proven to be inadequate. These two
factions, the proponents of moral force versus the advocates of physi-
cal force, laid out the terms of a split which was never resolved.

At the height of the movement, Marx made a prediction which seemed to have placed him on the side of the moral force among the Chartists:

> ...Universal suffrage is the equivalent of political power for the working class of England, where the proletariat forms the large majority of the population, where, in a long, though underground civil war, it has gained a clear consciousness of its position as a class, and where even the rural districts know no longer any peasants, but only landlords, industrial capitalists (farmers) and hired labourers. The carrying of Universal Suffrage in England would be a far more socialistic measure than anything which has been honoured with that name on the Continent. Its inevitable result here is the political supremacy of the working class.[15]

Marx still believed that as late as 1872, when, in an address to the International Working Men's Association in the Hague, he reiterated the prediction made twenty years earlier, and even extended the forecast to some other countries.

But at the point where the working class had won the right to vote, its leading spokesmen became imbued with the parliamentary game, learned to play it with consummate skill, and settled for reforms which could be won gradually.

At the same time, it had become obvious to a growing section of the middle class that the working class was now a factor which had to be reckoned with, not only in the work place but also in the political arena. John Stuart Mill emerged in the 1840s as an advocate of what became known as the liberal-democratic school of thought, which proposed to bring the working class into politics, but in such a way that it could not, by its numerical majority, dominate all other classes in Britain. He wrote:

> Where there is identity of position and pursuits, there will also be identity of partialities, passions, and prejudices; and to give to any one set of partialities, passions, and prejudices, absolute power, without counter-balance from partialities, passions and prejudices of different sort, is the way to render the correction of any of these imperfections hopeless; to make one narrow mean type of human nature,

universal and perpetual; and to crush every influence
which tends to the further improvement of man's intellectual and moral nature.[17]

Unlike Marx, however, Mill believed that the working class would
be prepared to share power with the other classes, providing these
classes would agree to conciliate:

I do not say that the working men's view of these questions is in general nearer to the truth than the other, but it
is something quite as near; and in any case it ought to be
respectfully listened to instead of being, as it is, not merely
turned away from, but ignored.[18]

Mill made a study of the growth of the socialist idea in Europe and
concluded that unless the British working class was brought into
political society, socialism would take root there too. The institution
of private property, he declared, is on trial and it must show that it is
capable of doing "more and better than it has hitherto done."[19] Mill
berated the British capitalists and the politicians for neglecting and
resisting demands of the working class for an improvement in its
conditions of life and labour:

...though for these reasons individual property has pre-
sumably a long term before it, if only of provisional existence, we are not, therefore to conclude that it must exist
during the whole term unmodified, or that all the rights
now regarded as appertaining to property, belong to it
inherently, and must endure while it endures. On the contrary, it is both the duty and interest of those who derive
the most direct benefit from the laws of property, to give
impartial consideration to proposals for rendering those in
ways less onerous to the majority.[20]

Mill put forward a pluralist view of Britain, in which all segments
of the people would advance their own proposals and in the ensuing
debate a consensus would emerge:

Unless opinions favourable to democracy and to aristocracy, to property and equality, cooperation and competition, to luxury and abstinence, to sociality and

individuality, to liberty and discipline, and all other standing antagonisms of practical life, are expressed with equal
talent and energy, there is no chance of both elements
obtaining their due.[21]

   Mill's theories did influence an ever widening circle of political
thinkers and activists in all camps, including many in the camp of
social-democracy. They would accept the Marxist idea that the class
interests of workers and capitalists were irreconcilable, but they
viewed this as a long-term proposition, which did not exclude the
possibility of compromise and conciliation at any given period.
   Although Marx and Engels spent most of their adult lives in Britain
and based their studies primarily on British political economy, they
did not exercise the degree of influence they enjoyed in continental
Europe. Nevertheless, important figures in the trade union movement
and left-wing intellectuals acknowledged in some measure the importance to them of the Marxist doctrine. Sidney Webb and William
Clarke used a good deal of Marx's economics in their essays for the
Fabian Society,[22] and Webb acknowledged the impact of Engels's
book, *Condition of the Working Class in England*.[23] George Bernard
Shaw paid tribute to the enormous influence Marx's *Capital* had on
him.[24] Other prominent intellectuals, such as William Morris, Henry
Hyndman, Belfort Bax, and Robert Blatchford, who already considered themselves socialists, admired Marx's writings but rejected
his theories of revolution, which embodied the idea that the capitalist
state would have to be overthrown and replaced by a state based on
the "dictatorship of the proletariat."
   The break between Marx and the English trade union leaders, who
sat with him in London on the General Council of the International
Workingmen's Association, erupted out of his Address to the Paris
Commune, which he called "the political form...under which to work
out the economical emancipation of Labour."[25] According to him, the
most important lesson to be learned from the Commune was that "the
working class cannot simply lay hold of the ready-made State
machinery, and wield it for its own purposes" but has to replace it
with an entirely new apparatus of rule."[26]
   The idea that the state is an instrument of class oppression which
might be overthrown by force and violence was not accepted by the
majority of trade union leaders in Britain. They believed that the state
was neutral and was there to protect whichever parliamentary government was in power. The fact that labour was already winning conces-

sions in the political and economic fields strengthened their belief in the impartiality of the state. British socialism, by the end of the nineteenth century, was founded on a profound belief in that neutrality.

This is repeatedly expressed in Ramsay MacDonald's book *Socialism and Society*, published in 1905. The days of the antagonistic confrontation of classes are over, he declared, and, with the winning of adult male suffrage, the characteristics of the state are transformed:

> For the State, after a democratic suffrage has been established, is no longer an authority external to the individual, a law is no longer a decree imposed upon the people by an arbitrary will bending a common will to its desires. The democratic State is an organization of the people, democratic government is self-government, democratic law is an expression of the will of the people.[27]

Marx's ideas, MacDonald declared, were applicable during the period up to the middle of the nineteenth century, but were now clearly obsolete. The proletarian revolution as predicted by Engels and Marx did not take place. Instead, the working class won many concessions through political pressure:

> Neither Marx nor Engels saw deep enough to discover the possibilities of peaceful advance which lay hidden beneath the surface. Their analogies misled them. Their German historical evolution and predominant school of philosophy, misled them. The continent — particularly Germany — unsettled by war, and by unnatural partitions was revolutionary; England was growing slowly and naturally bound into a social unity and well organized as a community in spite of the fearful social disintegration caused by the earlier stages of capitalism and production under factory conditions, was evolutionary.[28]

British capitalism, continuing its expansion at home and firmly set on a new wave of imperialist advance abroad, was able to concede a measure of reform for the benefit of the working class and thus avoid serious challenges from that quarter. There were conflicts on the way, but they were always kept within the system. At the end, paradoxically, it did not produce a strengthened Liberal Party, but a Labour Party that eventually would push aside the Liberals.

The Fabian Society probably played the key role in bringing this about. Its meetings and classes, its pamphlets, and above all the *Fabian Essays in Socialism*, provided the theoretical framework for a political party based on labour, just at a time when the labour movement, already tied to the Liberals, was seeking independence and freedom of political action.

The writings of Sidney Webb were especially important in providing the theoretical justification for the eventual formation of a Labour Party. His main work in this regard was *Socialism in England*, published in 1889.

The influence of John Stuart Mill is clearly seen in this book:

> Whilst recognizing Marx's valuable services to economic history, and a stirrer of men's minds, a large number of English Socialist Radicals reject his special contributions to pure economics…The economic influence most potent among Socialist Radicals is still that of John Stuart Mill.[29]

British socialists like Webb rejected the Marxist path of revolution based on irreconcilable class antagonisms, and adopted instead a demand for a greater share in the national income, more humane conditions of work and of life, and sharing of political power rather than proletarian rule.Webb claimed that this approach had already produced much legislation which he called socialist. In fact, Webb insisted that legislation which in any way ameliorates the living conditions of the worker is socialist. The body of factory legislation from 1832 on was socialist because,

> Innumerable restrictions upon the free use of private property, and the rights of ownership are thereby, in the public interest, considerably curtailed.[30]

He writes further about the development of municipalities, sewage systems, sanitation, and gas distribution as "municipal socialism."[31] He calls public education in England "socialism":

> In England…the rapid progress towards free government schools is rightly sighted as a marked instance of Socialist progress. The increased absorption of the incomes of the

comparatively rich, to provide for the education of their poorer brethren, makes its Socialist character disagreeably obtrusive to the capitalist as well as to the private school proprietor.[32]

He then lists four pages of functions which are being performed by the national and local governments as socialist, including the army, navy, police, post office, parks, museums, public baths, theatres, slaughter houses, cemeteries, street lighting, roads, bridges, etc.[33]

It will be objected by many persons that this is not what they understand by Socialism. There are doubtless still some who might be compelled to admit that they imagined that Socialists wanted to bring about a sanguinary conflict in the streets, and then next day to compel all delicately nurtured people to work at a fixed rate of wages in the government factories. This, however, is merely part of the obstinate survival of the "Utopian" conception of Socialism already referred to. Whether we so describe them or not, these features of modern English society are utterly contrary to the Individualist principles lately dominant in thought.[34]

This concept of Socialism, which Webb and other members of the Fabian Society expounded, became the dominant British view as preached and practised by the Labour Party. All notions of "class war" introduced at conferences and congresses of the Labour Representation Association and its successor, the Labour Party, were regularly voted down. If, therefore, one can speak of a British view of socialism, it could be as laid out in *The Fabian Essays in Socialism*, published in 1889:

It [the Fabian Society — N.P.] aims at the reorganization of society by the emancipation of land and industrial capital from individual and class ownership, and the vesting of them in the community for the general benefit...The Society accordingly works for the extinction of property in land...and for the transfer to the community of the administration of such industrial capital as can be conveniently managed socially...For the attainment of these ends the Fabian Society looks to the spread of socialist opinions, and the social and political changes consequent thereon.[35]

George Bernard Shaw, one of the founders of the Fabian Society, described its aim as follows:

> It was in 1885 that the Fabian Society amid the jeers of the catastrophists [Shaw means here the revolutionists — N.P.] turned its back on the barricades and made up its mind to turn heroic defeat into prosaic success. We set ourselves two definite tasks: first, to provide a parliamentary program for a Prime Minister converted to Socialism as Peel was converted to Free Trade; and second, to make it easy and matter-of-course for the ordinary respectable Englishman to be a Socialist as to be a Liberal or a Conservative.[36]

The Fabian Society used the word "permeation" to describe the gradual passage from capitalism to socialism by reforms rather than a revolutionary leap from one social system to another. The Essays, eclectic in character, list the kind of reforms required, backed up by a strong critique of capitalism and individualism, much of it taken from Marx.

In his essay, Sidney Webb stated that this gradual evolution to socialism is a combination of the political principles of liberal democracy in the field of government, with the principles of socialism in the economic field. Thus, in his view, British socialism became a compromise between liberalism and socialism, between individualism and collectivism, as was the compromise by John Stuart Mill in merging liberalism and democracy. One might add that Burke's strong advocacy of gradual rather than revolutionary change as the British road was taken over a century later to apply to a socialist path, and thus remaining within the British tradition. Shaw saw this as a reaction to the violence of the Paris Commune as well as the resiliency of the British middle class.

Thus the Fabians implanted the idea of the British path to socialism as a long-term goal, arrived at by improving the present society. To the extent that these reforms are brought about by the actions of the working class, this class begins more and more to become a political force of great importance in British politics. Engels, in his book *The Condition of the Working Class in England*, published in 1844, could

see fifty years earlier that this might become the characteristic feature
of socialism in Britain:

> English Socialism arose with Owen, a manufacturer, and
> proceeds therefore with great consideration toward the
> bourgeoisie and great injustice toward the proletariat in its
> method although it culminates in demanding the abolition
> of class antagonism between bourgeoisie and proletar-
> iat...The Socialists are thoroughly tame and peaceable,
> accept our existing order, bad as it is, so far as to reject
> all other methods but that of winning public opinion.[37]

British socialism in its dominant form did not represent a break
with the existing political culture, as an acceptance of Marxism would
have entailed. One of the reasons for this was the existence of a
radical wing of the middle class and its theorists, who, as indicated
above, sought the support of the working class at a time when this
section of the bourgeoisie was itself disenfranchised. British socialism could find much in the propaganda of the radicals and even
among the liberal democrats that reflected its own aspirations for the
working class.

The eventual merging of the Fabians with the labour movement
meant the rejection of Marxism, even though Marxism was not itself
barred from the Labour Party. The rejection of Marxism in Britain
was parallelled in the European socialist parties by the emergence of
a revisionism that also emphasized reformism, but kept Marxism in
their program.

The working-class immigrants who came to Canada from Britain
during the great wave of immigration in the first two decades of this
century included many who were to the left of the Labour Party and
the Trades Union Congress, and were more Marxist than Fabian. It
was not until after the First World War that Fabianism began to forge
ahead in Canadian socialist ranks, and it was only with the formation
of the CCF and the League for Social Reconstruction that Fabianism
became the central theme of Canadian social democracy.

Social democracy as an anti-capitalist ideology developed in the
nineteenth century, principally in the western European countries,
which were rapidly becoming industrialized. It developed out of a
critique of capitalist production, distribution, and exchange, which,
according to Arnold Toynbee, laid the foundation for a new branch
of economic science.[38] It developed out of the conditions of exploi-

tation manifest everywhere in the factories, and in the conditions which prevailed around them in the slums. Although the socialist idea was rapidly growing at this time, it was hardly doctrinaire, perhaps because it was too early for that. Young intellectuals were in the forefront of these debates, but they were joined by workers, skilled and unskilled, in trying to understand the nature of capitalism, and how to respond to it. But the main characteristic of political life in these countries at that time was the birth and growth of mass movements such as the Chartist and the trade union movements, as well as political parties based on the working class. A perceptive analysis described it this way:

> The movements to which the term socialism applies have been so diverse in starting-point and in goal, so variously colored by individual experience and social environment, so that the common element is often difficult to discern....It is a living movement, changing insensibly with every change in the mental horizon or material conditions of the time, and so impossible to label with the cheerful finality with which the scientist treats a paleolithic fossil.[39]

This was written in 1910, by Oscar D. Skelton, a Canadian economist, who later became a close colleague and adviser to Mackenzie King. According to this book, the socialist movement, world-wide, had over eight million voters, the majority of whom supported parties that followed the Marxist doctrine, even though their interpretations varied. The Socialist International brought these parties together for regular consultations, but it rarely adopted positions by majority vote that would compel all sections to comply.

What then were the common elements that seemed to unite in ideology, if not in action, the labour and socialist movements in the nineteenth century? According to Skelton they were "an indictment of any and all industrial systems based on private property and competition;" "an analysis of capitalism;" "a substitute for capitalism;" "and a campaign against capitalism."[40]

But these concepts did not appear suddenly and fully formed. They developed out of the class struggle, in the factories and workshops, in the campaign for working-class political rights, and in the writings and debates among intellectuals.

It was out of these actions that the words used to describe the overall aims of the new movements — socialism, communism, co-operative commonwealth, and social democracy — came into use. So too did the demands, both of an immediate and long-term nature: democracy (which meant votes for the propertyless); the eight-hour day; safeguards for child labour; centralization of credit, transportation, and vital industries in the hands of the state; extension of rights and laws protecting the trade unions; free education for all children in public schools; and nationalization of the land. But these demands, which today are taken for granted, were opposed by the establishment parties, Liberal and Conservative.

The rise of direct action on a factory or trade basis heralded the beginnings of trade unions in politics, which eventually became the main electoral base of social democracy. In Britain, while there were trade unions here and there from the beginning of the nineteenth century, the major thrust of the working class had been political rather than economic. The Chartist movement, which lasted almost twenty years from 1830 to 1850, campaigned for the right to vote and, at its height, mobilized millions of workers, most of whom were not members of trade unions because at that time few of them were in existence. After the passage of the Reform Act of 1867, which granted the vote to a substantial portion of the adult male workers, centre stage shifted to the trade unions, which began to take over as the mass organization of the working class.

The first congress of British trade unions took place two years later and, from that date on, the trade unions in Britain began to enrol hundreds of thousands of members.

However, there were schisms within the trade unions and within the Trades Union Congress over such issues as organizing the unorganized and the extent and nature of trade union involvement in politics. But, above all, there was an ongoing debate over the question of whether trade unions should adopt socialism in their union constitutions.

The dominant leaders at the founding congress in 1869, and for sometime after, favoured a political alliance between labour and the Liberal Party under William Gladstone. This arrangement worked for a while, resulting in the election of a number of trade union leaders under the Liberal-Labour banner. But as the trade union movement grew, especially in the mass industries such as mines, docks, and textile factories, there developed a new wave of radicalism, and simultaneously a new pressure for independent labour political action. Socialist parties, such as the Social-Democratic Federation, which was openly Marxist, the Fabian Society, and the Independent Labour

Party, came into existence to press for a break from the Liberal-Labour alliance, and this was consummated in the birth of the Labour Party in 1906.

Throughout the latter half of the nineteenth century, various movements, organizations, and journals appeared in Europe and America involving the working class. They included trade unions, co-operatives, political parties, and educational circles, expressing an alternative ideology, distinctive programs (both political and economic), and, almost simultaneously, a new and controversial theoretical outlook to guide what had begun as an amorphous and spontaneous development. The words "socialism" or "social-democratic" became interchangeable as terms most widely used to characterize these movements, and Karl Marx began to emerge as

> the greatest name on the roll of socialism. For half a century his theories have been the intellectual backbone of the movement, and whatever modifications and more or less ingenuous re-interpretations they have undergone these later days, it is still his personality which dominates the minds of millions of his fellow men ... The service of Marx to his cause, his followers claim, was to make socialism scientific, inevitable, proletarian, aggressive, international.[41]

Marx was an activist in the growing socialist movement in Germany, France, and Britain. Working together with Frederick Engels, he published *The Communist Manifesto* in 1848, which outlined a new kind of socialism. Engels's book *The Condition of The Working Class in England* was a brilliant exposé of the impact of the Industrial Revolution on the people who were forced to bear the major burdens of the rise of the factory system. In many ways this book inspired Marx, who had not met Engels, to study political economy rather than philosophy. The conclusion which Engels drew from his own study was that the condition of the proletariat in England was inevitably leading it to a growing class consciousness:

> But, in general, all the workers employed in manufacture are won for one form or the other of resistance to capital and bourgeoisie; and all are united upon this point, that they, as working-men, a title of which they are proud, and which is the usual form of address in Chartist meetings,

form a separate class, with separate interests and principles, with a separate way of looking at things in contrast
with that of all property-owners; and that in this class
reposes the strength and the capacity of development of
the nation.[42]

The defeat of the Chartist movement after the petition campaign
in 1848 was a temporary setback. The emphasis in working-class
action switched to trade union activity, to the organization of unions,
to securing factory legislation, and to obtaining laws to protect trade
unions. This activity led to the formation of the Trades Union Congress in 1869, which began to act as a co-ordinating centre for legislative matters affecting the unions. But because two years earlier the
House of Commons under Benjamin Disraeli's Conservatives had
extended the suffrage to a majority of adult male workers, the leaders
of the newly-formed Trades Union Congress entered into political
alliances with one or more of the existing parliamentary parties, in
order to exchange working-class votes for some particular reform
which was uppermost at the time. But, as elsewhere in western
Europe, the working class in Britain felt the need for a political party
of its own or one that it would dominate, and by 1906 the British
Labour Party was born. Soon, such parties, which challenged the
existing ones, had been founded in almost every country in western
Europe.

The British Labour Party, however, had some basic differences
with the European parties. It was not Marxist or even socialist at the
time of its foundation, and this was due mainly to the objections of
the trade union bureaucracy, who wanted to adhere to a strictly reform
program. But since the Labour Party was a federated one, some of its
adherents, such as the Fabian Society and the Independent Labour
Party, were explicitly socialist, while the Social-Democratic Federation, which withdrew shortly after the founding conference, was or at
least declared itself to be Marxist. Nevertheless, in 1907 the Labour
Party joined the Socialist International, but only after a vigorous
debate in which Karl Kautsky from the Social-Democratic Party of
Austro-Hungary, and Lenin from the Russian Social-Democratic
Labour Party, urged its acceptance.

By this time the Socialist International had among its members the
German, Austrian, French, and British mass parties and smaller parties such as the Russian, which was for most of the time underground,
and the American Socialist Labor Party. The congresses of the So-

cialist International were thus marked by vigorous and often bitter and acrimonious debates, especially among the parties which called themselves Marxist.

By the outbreak of the War of 1914-1918, the trade union movement and the political parties that were associated with it were strong and powerful, at least in the major capitalist countries, except for the United States. In these countries the alternative programs and the parties that advocated them were in place. Liberalism, which was the ideology of the rising bourgeoisie, and which by the beginning of the nineteenth century had been modified as a result of the working-class fight for democracy, was now challenged by labourism and socialism, both of which were defined by the term "social-democratic."

It was the philosophy of the British left, which in its majority was Fabian rather than Marxist, that eventually became the dominant outlook of Canadian social democracy.

2

The Agrarian Revolt
Revisited (1900–1930)

In 1911, a book entitled *The Revolt in Canada Against The New Feudalism* appeared and fueled the fires that were already burning among the farmers from coast to coast.[1] It became almost compulsory reading for the farmers' movements because it provided ammunition for the fight against high tariffs which had been in place since 1879, and which had become the main issue of the general election then in progress.

Since 1896, with the victory of Wilfrid Laurier and the Liberals, politics revolved around the contest between them and the Conservatives, but with respect to protectionism there had been no contest, at least in the farmers' view: both parties were protectionist at the behest of the manufacturers, banks, and railroad tycoons. Badgered by constant and escalating pressure by the farmers, the Liberal government had finally made a significant move away from high tariffs by signing a reciprocity treaty with the United States president, William Taft. The Conservatives made this the issue in the campaign, and won.

The revolt of the farmers, far from subsiding after the defeat of reciprocity and the Liberal government, grew considerably and appeared to be heading for the establishment of a farmers' party, but this was interrupted by the 1914–1918 World War in which Canada, a colony of Great Britain, was a major participant.

During the first thirty years after Confederation, with one exception, the Liberals occupied the provincial governments and the Conservatives, the federal. Thus at the first meeting of provincial premiers, which took place in Quebec City, November 1887, the five premiers present were Liberals[2] — New Brunswick, Nova Scotia, Ontario, Manitoba and Quebec — and the two absentees were British Columbia and Prince Edward Island, both Conservative governments. When Alberta and Saskatchewan became provinces in 1905, they started off with Liberal governments, but by this time there was a Liberal government in Ottawa, under Sir Wilfrid Laurier. This was the beginning of the two-party system in both federal and provincial politics, with the names of the parties and the governmental system copied from the British.

But while there were similarities with Canada, there were also real differences: federal union, as contrasted with the British legislative union; the existence of two nations, French and English-speaking; two unofficial state religions — Roman Catholic ultramontanism and the Church of England; government funding of social and private capital, thus creating an indigenous capitalist class; and millions of acres of cheap or free land, offered to people from Britain, the United States, and, eventually, Europe.

It was the settling of this unused land — first in Ontario, followed by massive immigration into the Canadian West — that produced a new class of small entrepreneurs who created powerful farmers' movements with a populist outlook, and new political parties that eventually left the two-party system in shambles.

The farm organizations began as social centres in the rural wilderness, developing into institutions of collective self-help, drawing up grievances which were presented to municipal, provincial, and federal governments. Simultaneously, they opened co-operative establishments to market their products.

At the outset, most of the farmers' organizations were branches of American ones, such as the Patrons of Industry and the Patrons of Husbandry, often called the Grange. It was this organization that entered the Ontario provincial elections in 1894 and unexpectedly elected 17 candidates in a Legislature of 94.

Although this electoral victory was not repeated until 1919, the farmers did not forget this episode, which had shown the possibilities of an independent partisan political force. It was the growing political awareness of the farmers in Ontario and in the West that eventually brought about the replacement of the American movements by farmers' organizations on a provincial basis, with a Canadian Council of Agriculture co-ordinating the activities at the federal level. By the end of the second decade of this century the most powerful of the farmers' organizations were the United Farmers of Ontario (UFO), the United Farmers of Manitoba (UFM), the Saskatchewan Grain Growers' Association (SGGA), the United Farmers of Alberta (UFA), and the Canadian Council of Agriculture (CCA).

These organizations published hard-hitting weekly journals, such as *The Farmers' Sun*, and *The Grain Growers' Guide*, supplemented by several books which were studied regularly at meetings of the branches: *Progress and Poverty* by Henry George,[3] *History of Canadian Wealth* by Gustavus Myers,[4] *The Revolt in Canada Against The New Feudalism* by Edward Porritt,[5] and *Canada To-Day* by J. A. Hobson.[6]

They were in the front ranks of a general reform movement that was making itself felt in the western world in the first period of the twentieth century:

> In the first decade of the century a general reform movement had also been growing in the Canadian West. In its early stages at least, the farmers' movement was indeed only one, though a major, part of the general movement, a fact which often served to veil its agrarian and sectional character. The general reform movement itself was at core a demand for positive state action with respect to such matters as the prohibition of the sale of alcoholic liquor, the promotion of social welfare, and the cleansing of political life. This reform sentiment was most active in the West, as a region of recent immigration and acute political grievances, in which a native conservatism had scarcely begun to develop.[7]

The industrial revolution sweeping Europe, Britain, and North America, resulted in slum cities, harsh working conditions, child and female sweated labour, unemployment, and extremes of rich and poor. The response to these conditions was the growth of the trade union and labour movement, liberal and social reform movements, socialism, and agrarian populism.

James Shaver Woodsworth, a divinity student at the University of Toronto doing graduate work in 1900 at Oxford, spent ten months in the slums of London. He would later emerge as a leader in the social gospel movement in Winnipeg during the war, and one of the leaders of the Winnipeg General Strike in 1919. William Lyon Mackenzie King, at the turn of the century, did his M.A. thesis at the University of Chicago on the conditions in the packinghouses of that city.[8] Oscar

Skelton wrote his Ph. D. dissertation on "Socialism" at Harvard in 1910, and later teamed up with Mackenzie King to become a reformer within the Liberal Party.[9] In 1913, Skelton, then a professor at Queen's University in Kingston, wrote an economic history of Canada in which he made this indictment of Canadian capitalism:

> ...inequality grew due rather to the more rapid enrichment of the few than to the impoverishment of the many; prosperity drove in a wedge between the well-to-do and the struggling. Montreal alone claimed seventy new millionaires in a decade. Where the millions corresponded to social service, where they were the fruit of daring pioneering in the opening up of new resources or the improvement of industrial processes, few grudged enterprise and energy their reward. But most men viewed with growing uneasiness the concentration of wealth in the hands that had done little towards its making, and the domination of industrial and political life by small groups of allied financial and railway and industrial interests in the three or four larger cities. Financial buccaneers who made millions out of merging mills they had never seen; promoters of fraudulent mines...[10]

The Grain Growers' Guide, from its inception in 1908, hammered incessantly at this theme, and in its special issue of June 25, 1913, devoted the entire contents to the question "Who Owns Canada?" Its answer was that forty-two men "control more than one-third of the wealth of the nation, aggregating over $4,000,000,000..."[11]

The *Guide* named them and their interconnections in banks, boards of directors, railways, and manufacturing. It called this group the "Triple Alliance of Banking, Railway, and Manufacturing interests...". They worked in close relationship with the government; they received subsidies for railway building; they received protection through high tariffs and high freight rates; and they set the interest rates and credit terms for the whole country:

> It is doubtful if ever before in the history of the world there has been such a concentration of the control of wealth in the hands of a few as exists in Canada today.

Reinforced by these revelations, the *Guide* listed the farmers' demands: the nationalization of the railways, telegraphs, telephones, and other public utilities; the removal of the protective tariff; the banks to be restricted from charging exorbitant interest rates; taxation of unimproved land; Direct Legislation, the implementation of the Initiative, Referendum and Recall; and female suffrage.

Most of these demands were presented at the so-called "Siege of Ottawa," which took place in December 1910, when over eight hundred delegates, representing farmers' organizations from every section of Canada, met the leaders of the government.[12]

In 1911, the British government asked Canada to contribute to the expansion of the British navy, and this demand stirred up a new controversy throughout the country in which the farmers' movement participated. The *Guide* conducted a referendum among its readers on a number of policy options and published the results in its edition of February 4, 1914. On the question of supporting or rejecting naval rearmament, the vote was overwhelmingly negative: men 348 for, 3,684 against; women: 445 for, 2,366 against.

A year before this referendum, the *Guide* published an article by E. C. Drury, then vice-president of the Canadian Council of Agriculture, and later to become the premier of Ontario, heading the first farmers' government in Canadian history:

> Once we participate in the naval defense of the Empire, it appears that we stand pledged to support Britain in all her wars — a virtual tribute, since we can have no real say in the making of peace or war — or to withhold our support at the peril of severing our connection.[13]

The farmers' movement took an anti-war position up to the outbreak of the war against Germany. *The Grain Growers' Guide* of August 5, 1914, carried this box on the cover:

THE DEMON OF WAR

> The war demon is abroad in Europe and thousands of men are engaged in the slaughter of their fellow men. Those who ordered the war will be comfortably located far beyond the danger zone, but homes will be desolated, crops destroyed, children orphaned, fathers and sons killed and maimed, wives and mothers left to mourn their dead

and rear their families alone. Is Canada to be forced
blindly and needlessly into this horrible struggle.[14]

But in the next issue, August 12, the box on the cover proclaimed
"British Ideals Must Triumph...Canada has everything at stake and
must stand by Britain to the very limit of our resources. In self defence
we must do our utmost in the struggle in which Britishers everywhere
are now engaged."[15]

Within a few weeks' time, however, fissures began to appear
which modified the initial enthusiasm for the war. British ideals, the
Guide suggested, may not be strong enough to prevent the practice
of discrimination against Canadian citizens who were born in Germany or in the Austro-Hungarian Empire (which covered a number
of East European countries), from which many hundreds of thousands
of immigrants had come after 1900 at the invitation of the Canadian
government. Notwithstanding this warning, discrimination against
these immigrants was rampant, by individuals, organizations, employers, the police, and the government itself. "Foreigners," as they
were called, were fired, the Wartime Elections Act deprived them of
their right to vote, thousands were interned, and foreign language
periodicals were banned.

Before the end of 1915, evidence was mounting which showed
excess profiteering by Canadian manufacturers in supplying food,
clothing, and arms to the war effort. Moreover, a considerable amount
of these supplies were defective. The farmers' press, and especially
The Grain Growers' Guide, lost no time in publishing these stories,
and demanding action against those found guilty.

The decision of the Conservative government of Robert Borden
and later of the Union government to conscript able-bodied men for
the armed forces became the major issue of Canadian politics. The
farmers vehemently opposed this policy initially, on the grounds that
it would take away men who were needed to produce the food for the
war, but changed their attitude when, during the 1917 election campaign, the Union candidates assured them that the government would
be generous in granting exemptions to farmers and their sons. However, a few months after the victory of the Union government, the
prime minister announced that, because of the critical situation on the
Western Front, his government could not fulfill this promise.

The issue of conscription in the early part of 1917 divided Canada,
not only between French and English but also within the farmers' and
labour movements. At the Thirty-third Annual Convention of the

Trades and Labour Congress of Canada, the delegates voted by a narrow margin of 111-101 not to oppose conscription. The "minority" would have had the TLC on record not to support conscription unless wealth was conscripted first.[16]

This demand became a slogan of the left in the labour movement as well as in the farmers' organizations. But with the determined pressure being exerted among western Liberals, particularly by J. W. Dafoe, editor of the *Manitoba Free Press*, a number of prominent farmers' leaders supported the Union government, and the most important, T. A. Crerar, president of the United Grain Growers of Manitoba, accepted the post of Agriculture in the Union cabinet, although he had never held an elective office before. But Henry Wise Wood, president of the United Farmers of Alberta (UFA), refused a similar invitation. *The Grain Growers' Guide* campaigned against the Union government, suspicious that it would renege on its promise of generous exemptions.

The conflict on the conscription issue temporarily slowed the drive for a farmers' party, but the effort to involve the farmers in independent politics resumed immediately after Borden announced, in April 1918, that he was revoking his promise of generous exemptions for farm men. The farmers were outraged and staged protest rallies across the country, culminating in a special convention in Toronto's Massey Hall, on June 7, 1918, with more than 3,000 in attendance, and characterized as "the most tumultuous gathering in the long annals of Canadian agrarian history." [17]

Not all the agrarian spokesmen felt outraged. Crerar was in favour of conscription, and hostile to the French Canadians. He quit the Borden cabinet in June 1919, and then established a bloc of ten MPs from rural constituencies who also quit the Conservative-Liberal Union ranks. It was by then clear that the decision to set up a new party had been made, and was irreversible.

There were important differences within the farmers' ranks, but the party was launched without resolving them and, in fact, they were never resolved.

For years the farmers had been critical of the party system as it operated in Canada, and this criticism began to permeate the labour movement as well. One of the most effective labour critics was Fred J. Dixon, who had been elected to the Manitoba Legislature in 1914 as a candidate of the Dominion Labour Party. His speech on the subject of electoral reform, which he called "Direct Legislation," was considered a classic and was printed in *The Grain Growers' Guide* of March 24, 1915.

The phrase "Direct Legislation" embodied the process of "Initiative, Referendum, and Recall," by which legislation would be initiated at the constituency level, introduced in Parliament, and if defeated would be submitted to the voters in a referendum. It would also include the right of the electors in any riding to recall their sitting member if his work in the legislature was unsatisfactory to them.[18] Dixon was also a strong advocate of women's suffrage, as was most of the farmers' movement.

A variation of this was the concept of "group government," which had been proposed by Henry Wise Wood, president of the United Farmers of Alberta, and supported by William Irvine, a colleague of J. S. Woodsworth, and author of *The Farmers in Politics*, which was first published in 1920. According to Wood, legislation should be the result of the coming together of representatives of the major economic groups, rather than through political parties, which pretend that they are above economic interest. Wood advocated co-operation between farmers and labour rather than merging them in a farmer-labour party. J. S. Woodsworth, who spent much of 1918 in Alberta organizing the Non-Partisan League with William Irvine, believed in a "peoples' party" rather than group government. But before they had an opportunity to debate these ideas, a provincial election was called in Ontario in October 1919, with the United Farmers of Ontario winning 43 seats, the Independent Labour Party 12, Liberals 28, Conservatives 26, and 2 independents.[19] This was followed by an election in July 1921 in Alberta, with the United Farmers of Alberta winning 37 seats and Labour 4, out of a total of 61.

These elections took the country by surprise, and that included the people who were directly involved. Yet there had been many signs of discontent during and following the end of the war in various places throughout Canada as well as Europe. Beginning with the two revolutions in Russia in 1917, the spirit of rebellion against the rulers, no matter who they were, was spreading. In Canada, the major manifestation of this unrest was the 1919 Winnipeg General Strike, which left the third largest city in the country paralyzed from May 21 to June 26, and which was followed by almost a year of state trials of the strike leaders.

Although the farmers' movements pledged their support for the war effort, they did not call off their demands, particularly their bitter opposition to the high tariff policy of Borden's Conservative government. While their stand on conscription was divided at the outset, it changed decisively after the government reneged on its solemn promise to give generous exemptions to the farmers and their sons. After the defeat of reciprocity, the movement among the farm organizations towards a new party accelerated, starting with E. A. Partridge's pamphlet of 1913 called *The No-Party League,* and involving advocates of group government, Direct Legislation, a people's party, and a farmer-labour party. But while the movements were directed at federal policies, the first victories of the new farmer parties were in Ontario and Alberta. In Ontario, a coalition of farmer and labour groups had the majority in the Legislature; in Alberta a farmers' party won the elections, but worked with a four-member group from labour. In December 1921, the biggest victory of all took place when the Progressive Party elected sixty-five members to become the second largest party in the House of Commons.

These were heady days, but there were also problems to be faced. The sixty-five MPs were united around a minimum platform, and were able to find common ground with the two-man labour group, J. S. Woodsworth and William Irvine, who had been elected for the first time. But since they were independent, lacking a common program, there were bound to be differences as well as similarities in their presentations to the House and in committees.

While the victories in the two provincial elections were unexpected, so too were the sixty-five seats won by the Progressive Party in the general elections, four months after the United Farmers of Alberta had become the government of that province. On the other hand, the election of only two labour candidates was a major disappointment, since expectations for these candidates had been much higher, with "fifteen to twenty members" being predicted.[20]

The distribution of the seats won by the Progressives was even more surprising: New Brunswick 1, Ontario 24, Manitoba 12, Saskatchewan 15, Alberta 11, and British Columbia 2. Six out of nine provinces elected members of the new party, with Ontario electing the most: 24 seats elected with a total vote of 314,092, on par with the votes for the Conservatives and Liberals. Saskatchewan and Alberta, the two provinces that were chartered in 1905, voted 53 percent and 61 percent respectively for the new party, demonstrating that the federal set-up made it easier to found and build parties different from the traditional parties.

But notwithstanding these features, the new party on the federal level, and the new parties on a provincial level, were from the beginning unstable, due to the wide assortment of ideologies on which they were based: populist, social-democratic, socialist, and liberal. All of them, however, were able to unite around the Farmers' Platform, which went through various alterations from 1910 to 1921. Its main thrust was for free trade, tax on unimproved land, graduated income tax, social legislation, direct legislation through the initiative, refer- endum, and recall, and opening seats in Parliament for women.[21]

There were no demands for nationalization of railways or other means of communication, or state control of banks and credit, which had been the theme of *The Grain Growers' Guide*, although there were Progressive MPs who believed in those measures, and who were ready to do battle against the so-called "Triple-Alliance." It was obvious that the leadership of the Progressive group in the House was dominated by members who had been card-carrying Liberals. The guiding light for these people was J. W. Dafoe, who had led the breakaway of western Liberals from Laurier in 1917 over the con- scription issue. T. A. Crerar, a close colleague of Dafoe, was per- suaded by him to become the leader of the Progressive bloc in Parliament, whatever its size. Crerar ran as a Progressive in 1921 in Marquette, where he was elected in 1917 on the Union Government ticket.

A revealing episode occurred at the last public meeting for Crerar in the 1921 election in his riding, when Oscar Skelton, then professor of Political Economy at Queen's, and a member of Mackenzie King's team, addressed the rally in support of Crerar, ignoring Lewis St. George Stubbs, the official Liberal candidate, who had been per- suaded by Mackenzie King to be the Liberal standard bearer there.[22]

Mackenzie King's strategy towards the Progressive and Labour members was to abstain from attacking them in order to win them back into the Liberal Party. He recognized them as fellow reformers and believed that he could work with them. On the other hand, J. S. Woodsworth, one of two Labour members, set out to convince the Progressives to join with Labour to establish a "people's party," with radical or even socialist policies.

Both succeeded to a certain extent, but another party, called the Social Credit League, surfaced in 1935, replacing the UFA in the provincial arena and the other parties in the federal field.

The reformers, and the reform movements, began making an im- pact in the first two decades of this century, advocating reform liber- alism, or labourism, or social democracy, or socialism. But it was not until after the war, amid the upheavals throughout Europe, that they emerged in the forefront of Canadian politics.

The major figure was Mackenzie King, who was elected leader of the Liberal Party in August 1919. He was little known outside party ranks in Ontario and Quebec, and "an unknown quantity" in the West.[23] But he had been Deputy Minister of Labour and Minister of Labour from 1901 until the defeat of Laurier's government in 1911. His book, which was published in 1918 under the title *Industry and Humanity*, was a blueprint for the welfare state in Canada. He utilized the Winnipeg General Strike, which took place a few months before the leadership convention, to show the necessity for liberal reformism. He formed a close relationship with like-minded Professor Oscar Skelton, who had spent the ten years from 1910 to 1920 advising the wealthy backers of the Liberal Party to support social legislation, and to do this in order to prove that capitalism performs better than socialism.

J. S. Woodsworth, William Irvine, and Salem Bland were to the left of the reformers in the Liberal Party. They had started out as ministers of the Protestant church and advocates of the Social Gospel; they formed close relations with the labour movement and the farm organizations, and actually started to organize a Non-Partisan League, a so-called "peoples' party" with a farmer-labour base.

Henry Wise Wood, president of the United Farmers of Alberta, was an early advocate of what he called "group government," which meant managing the country through the major economic groups such as farm, labour, manufacturer, rather than through parties. He never wavered from this concept, and because of that he opposed making the UFA a farmer-labour party. William Irvine's book *The Farmer in Politics,* published in 1920, explained the concept of group government.[24]

It is interesting and significant that the British Labour Party at a series of conferences in 1918 drew up a radical, in fact socialist, platform, entitled *Labour and the New Social Order*. This platform had an impact in Canada on the socialist organizations and many of their leaders, and also on reform-minded liberals such as Mackenzie King, who quoted from the literature of that party to support his "National Minimum Standard of Life." [25]

Woodsworth in his articles on a people's party, William Irvine in his book, and James Simpson, vice-president of the Trades and Labour Congress of Canada, all admired the new platform of the British Labour Party.

Woodsworth entered the House with a definite idea of what kind of party he wanted, using the parliamentary forum as the main vehicle, and the sixty-five farmer MPs as his immediate constituency. It was to be a people's party rather than a labour party. It would include workers, farmers, veterans, small business men, and intellectuals. In the first of seven articles, which appeared in *The Western Labor News*, August 23, 1918, he wrote on the subject, "Organizing Democracy in Canada":

> ...Now that the old parties have joined forces in a Union Government, it would seem that the democrats have a splendid opportunity to develop a genuine peoples' party in which farmers, industrial workers, returned soldiers, and progressives, could all find a place.[26]

The British Labour Party might be the model for many advocates of a new party, but, according to Woodsworth, the situation was different in Canada. The labour segment of the population in Canada was much smaller proportionately than in Britain, whereas the farmers here occupied a more strategic place from the demographic and political viewpoints. He insisted that no new party could be successful, or even formed, without a farmer and labour base, and that must be reflected in its program. Yet in his first article after the Winnipeg General Strike, he called for a socialist party:

> ...Our ultimate object must be the complete turnover in the present economic and social system. In this we recognize our solidarity with the workers the world over...This is frankly "revolutionary" but does not look at all in the direction of a violent bloody revolution...[28]

He reiterated that this must be the character of a genuinely new party and he had no doubt such a party could unite, "organized labor, farmers, returned men, and the 'progressives' among the middle classes of our towns and cities." [29]

In the subsequent three articles, Woodsworth outlined a detailed program that called for "socialization" of most of the big corporations, railways, and banks, and a program of social legislation to implement the idea that "human rights must come before property rights." [29]

Woodsworth never retreated from this program, and insisted that its basic themes and much of the wording be included in the Regina Manifesto fourteen years later at the founding convention of the Co-operative Commonwealth Federation. Independent and Dominion Labour Parties had come into existence in many of the larger urban centres from the beginning of the century, made up mostly of British working-class immigrants who had been members or supporters of similar party organizations in Britain. Socialist parties which proclaimed themselves Marxist movements had been established as well, actively promoting the socialist idea and the trade union movement. Most of these organizations had succeeded by 1917 in joining with the Trades and Labour Congress to found the Canadian Labour Party, but by 1927 it was evident that this organization would not succeed in replacing the two old parties, or the Progressive Party, which by then was declining.[30]

Woodsworth did not join either the Canadian Labour Party or the Progressives, although he maintained good relations with both. He was a member of the Manitoba Independent Labour Party, which he had joined in June 1921, on his return to Winnipeg, and which had decided, largely at his insistence, that the Canadian Labour Party was not the road to a genuine peoples' party.

By the end of the war the political system was in a shambles. The Union Government was a coalition of the ruling Conservatives and anglophone Liberals who had deserted their party on the conscription issue, but had no intention of staying with the Tories.

The Liberal Party, after the death of its leader, Sir Wilfrid Laurier, and sensing the mood of the nation, decided at its convention of August 1919 to adopt a reform program, and, by a narrow margin, to elect Mackenzie King as leader. King was the only leadership candidate that presented himself as a champion of reform, and received most of the Quebec votes because he had not supported conscription.

The Trades and Labour Congress, which had launched the Canadian Labour Party in 1917 but elected none of its candidates in the general election that year, was getting ready to try again. But it found the advocates of labour as an independent political force, or of a farmer-labour party, or a peoples' party, hopelessly divided over which option to take.

The Quebec voters had the least difficulty in deciding their immediate political future. The francophone Quebeckers had been isolated by the rest of Canada because of their opposition to compulsory military service in a war which was of little or no interest to them.

They would vote Liberal with Mackenzie King as leader because he was seen as a Laurier man.

But the most volatile debates on the future of Canadian party politics took place among the farmers, and it was clear from the outset that they wanted a new party with a radical platform that would express their agrarian interests, and which they would control.

Yet that did not cover all the issues that were in contention, most of which were subsumed by the argument between the advocates of group government and parliamentary government. Those who wanted group government were more left-wing and even socialist; most of those who controlled the federal party were liberals. The MPs from Alberta were devoted to the group concept; those from Ontario were divided, as were those from Saskatchewan, while the Manitoba MPs were liberals, influenced by J. W. Dafoe and T. A. Crerar.

It was E. C. Drury, the United Farmers premier of Ontario, who first used the term "broadening out" to describe the policy of extending the program and the people beyond the confines of the farmers' movement,[31] and it was Dafoe who campaigned in the western farm movement to have this concept replace the ideas of group government. In an editorial in the *Manitoba Free Press*, on December 15, 1922, he made his policy quite clear:

> The development towards broadening out is regarded with suspicion by many of the farmers... But so far as getting their programmes effectively applied the farmers have not got very far; and their political leaders — as distinguished from the preachers of class consciousness — are conscious that they will get no farther and they will probably lose some of the ground they now hold unless they make this movement the heart of a national political party to which the attainment of power will not be impossible.[32]

Dafoe, Crerar, and Drury, among others, wanted to transform the Progressive Party and its provincial counterparts into a peoples' party that would be moderate in its policies, so as to attract the middle class, and even members of the bourgeoisie. J. S. Woodsworth wanted a people's party which would centre on an alliance between the farmers and the industrial working class, and therefore would advocate radical, left-wing, and even socialist policies. Henry Wise Wood fought to maintain the "group government" concept, as did such left-wing farmers' leaders as E. A. Partridge, director of *The Grain Growers'*

Guide, out of Winnipeg, and J. J. Morrison, secretary of the United Farmers of Ontario.

The Canadian Labour Party too was looking for a place in the sun, but was ineffective. The Trades and Labour Congress, which was the official sponsor of the Canadian Labour Party, was made up of craft unions, and did not include the majority of workers, who were un- skilled and therefore outside the concern of the TLC. The TLC, as the official body of the American Federation of Labor in Canada, was bound to a certain extent to heed the non-partisan policy of the AFL, or at least recognize that many of the AFL unions in Canada would be prevented from affiliating to a political party, even one sponsored by the TLC.

There was undoubtedly hostility to the labour movement in the farmers' organizations. This was described in the history of that period in the *Agrarian Revolt in Western Canada*:

> Agrarian sympathy for organized labor was shocked into open hostility by the Winnipeg general strike of 1919...Most farmers believed the ready explanation that the ringleaders of the strike were foreign agitators, and the Manitoba jury of farmers which condemned three of the labor leaders to prison was applauded throughout the West.[33]

There is no doubt that the propaganda against the Winnipeg General Strike was accepted by a majority of farmers. It was well known that the Royal North-West Mounted Police and the "Com- mittee of 1000" spent over a million dollars on this propaganda, which included sending officers of the RNWMP to lecture throughout the province with its interpretation of the Winnipeg events, while the labour movement of Winnipeg was unable or neglected to counter with its side. The *Manitoba Free Press* under Dafoe, which had a wide circulation in rural Manitoba, added its voice daily to bolster the anti-strike and anti-labour propaganda already reaching the farmers.

But even at that, the farmers did not turn into a one-sided, anti- labour force. J. S. Woodsworth and Fred Dixon were both arrested for their participation and leadership of the strike, yet they were never regarded by the farmers as "trouble makers" or "agitators," and cer- tainly not as "foreign agents." A bill to change the character and scope of the RNWMP, by establishing the Royal Canadian Mounted Police as a dominion-wide force in October 1919, was made necessary, according to the Borden government, by the Winnipeg strike. Yet when Woodsworth moved a private members bill in April 1922 to return the RCMP to the pre-1919 status of the RNWMP, all the Progressives, including their leader T. A. Crerar, supported his motion. The Independent Labour Party of Ontario, which had supported the Winnipeg strike, was invited by the United Farmers of Ontario in October 1919 to join it in forming a farmer-labour government, which became the first and only farmer-labour government in Canadian history.

In an article dated October 15, 1928 in *The Country Guide* (the new name of *The Grain Growers' Guide*), the author paid this tribute to Woodsworth:

> Last but not least there is J. S. Woodsworth, the leader of the Labour group. The Commons is ready to listen to an honest advocate and gradually Mr. Woodsworth has gained ground until today he is one of the foremost members of the House.[34]

Moreover, Woodsworth by that time had become the acknowledged leader of the "Ginger Group," which consisted of twelve Progressives and two or three Labour members. This group remained under Woodsworth's guidance, acting as the parliamentary group of the Co-operative Commonwealth Federation prior to the official founding of that party in July 1933, and remaining in that capacity until the general election of 1935. Mackenzie King cultivated both the Progressive and Labour groups, but he never went any further than he felt compelled to in introducing any of the social measures in his book *Industry and Humanity*, or of his labour platform that was adopted at the Liberal leadership convention in 1919. His main achievement along these lines was the introduction in 1926, and eventual passage, of a Dominion-Provincial Old Age Pension Act, but this was due as much, if not more, to King's desperate need for the two votes of the labour group to keep him in office.[35]

King has been described as a pseudo-reformer on the basis of his record in this field. That record encompasses the eight years (1922–30) he occupied as prime minister, and the four times he led the Liberals in bitter elections. One account of that period interpreted Woodsworth's actions in this manner:

...but Woodsworth's action had aligned the Left in Canada with the Liberal Party as a lesser evil than the Conservative. King's early radicalism, generally forgotten, had built a tacit alliance which might save him now, and would certainly profit his Party in due season.[36]

King, with his predilection toward social reforms, made them the main theme of his platform at the leadership convention. But he also came to the convention as the only nominee who could appeal to the French Quebeckers, because of his support for Laurier's opposition to conscription, and thus won most of the delegates from Quebec. In the general election of December 1921, the Liberals won all sixty-five Quebec seats. The Roman Catholic hierarchy in Quebec made it quite clear, however, that under the British North America Act social measures belonged exclusively to the provinces. Moreover, most of the Liberal MPs, whether from Quebec or other provinces, found it convenient to utilize this aspect of federal-provincial relations to block any attempts King might have made to move social legislation from his book into statutes. When the House passed the Old Age Pension in 1926, and again in 1927 (because the Senate had vetoed the 1926 Act), it had to be passed as a federal-provincial cost-sharing project, since the Quebec Liberal government stated that it would not be participating in what it considered a federal usurpation of a basic provincial right, even though by not participating it would deprive poor Quebeckers over the age of 70 of a much-needed benefit.[37]

In his famous essay, "Conservatism, Liberalism, and Socialism in Canada: An Interpretation," first published in 1966, Gad Horowitz, an outstanding political theorist, made this observation:

> King's *Industry and Humanity* and the Liberal platform of 1919 mark the transition of English Canadian Liberalism from the old individualism to the new Liberal Reform.[38]

But history does not confirm this analysis. From the outset of his career as the Deputy-Minister of Labour, to which he was appointed in September 1900, until he returned to the House of Commons, this time as the leader of the Liberals, King had devoted most of his time to becoming the foremost expert on labour relations. It was during those years as Deputy and then Minister of Labour, and after that as labour adviser to several of the biggest industrialists in the United States, that he made a name for himself as labour conciliator, and reformer. But this was a far cry from making the Liberal Party, or the English section of it, into reformers. King was aware of the road that the Liberal Party would have to travel, but as long as there was no cohesive social-democratic party in existence there was no pressure for him to pass substantial reforms until he felt compelled to inaugurate an old age pension on penalty of losing a crucial vote of confidence.

The period from the end of World War I until the outbreak of the Great Depression was ushered in by the march on Ottawa in 1917, a continuation of the 1910 "Seige of Ottawa," the election of farmers' governments in Ontario and Alberta, and a new national farmers' party which elected sixty-five members to the House of Commons. But the different ideologies among members of the Progressive Party bloc in the House of Commons — radical populists, social democrats, socialists, and liberals — made it impossible for the party to accept the role of official opposition to which it was entitled. Instead, Mackenzie King and Woodsworth were competing with each other for their support. Some of the members joined the Liberal ranks, a smaller number constituted the "Ginger Group," which was social-democratic in its outlook. The failure of this period was the inability of the labour movement to create its own strong party, or to join in a farmer-labour party, with a social-democratic platform. The "agrarian revolt" was brief and militant, but before it subsided it had undermined the two-party system and opened the way for third parties.

3

Labour on the Road to Politics (1900–1930)

At the turn of the century, twenty-five years after Confederation, there were at least four identifiable sections of the population who were disaffected: the farmers, the industrial workers, the French Canadians, and the aboriginals.

The aboriginals had been defeated in the Red River Insurrection of 1870 and the North-West Rebellion of 1885, and would not rise again in militant struggle until late in the present century. The *canadiens*, who had been defeated in 1838, were beginning once again to assert their national rights in response to the demands of British imperialists that Canada supply manpower for their military adventures. The working class was just beginning to create trade unions and, alongside them, forms of independent political action. The farmers were the most vociferous and successful of the dissident groups in formulating their demands and in establishing organizations to fight for them.

The trade unions, like the farmers' organizations, were influenced by their American counterparts, and indeed at the outset most of them were extensions of the American Federation of Labor and the Knights of Labor. They were also influenced by the British Labour Party, which at this time was just coming into existence.[1] There was some support for the idea of a Canadian labour party, even at this early stage in the development of the trade unions. There were also small socialist groups, which preached the Marxist doctrine, and which were made up mostly of trade unionists.

However, the idea of launching a labour political party at this time appeared unrealistic. The labour movement was very small, and poorly organized. The trade unions affiliated to the AFL were craft types, and the Knights of Labor, which had organized unskilled workers particularly in Quebec, was being attacked by the Catholic hierarchy in that province, and by the AFL. The socialist groups were not ready for independent politics that would unite the workers on a broad non-doctrinaire platform. They advocated a socialist rather than a labour party, considering the latter to be a betrayal of the working-class interest.

Samuel Gompers, head of the AFL, was opposed to the trade unions forming their own party, although he did participate in some uniquely labour struggles, such as the election campaign of Henry George for mayor of New York.[2] His main objection to a labour party was that it would be turned into a socialist party.

The conditions that produced a labour party in Britain stood in sharp contrast to those in Canada. The British labour movement already had strong trade unions, including craft and unskilled mass production unions, co-operative societies, an Independent Labour Party, several Marxist groups, a Fabian society, and a parliamentary bloc. It had a century-long tradition of struggle for the right to vote, and of testing the advances made for the labour vote by both Conservatives and Liberals, and decided that it needed a party that would represent the working class first. Moreover, the working class was the majority of the British population; there was a large number of constituencies, in which workers made up the overwhelming body of the electorate.

Although Marx, in 1852, expressed the view that working-class suffrage would mean working-class power, the majority of the workers did not vote immediately for the British Labour Party. Nevertheless, in the first general election in which fifty candidates stood for this party, twenty-nine were elected, and the party has never looked back.[3]

On the other hand, the labour movement in the United States grew rapidly at the end of the last century, especially after the Civil War had given a tremendous boost to the expansion of manufacturing, railroads, shipping, mining, logging, cotton, clothing, and consumer goods. But at the very outset, the American unions developed differently than those in Britain. They grew under three or more centres, such as the American Federation of Labor, the Knights of Labor, the American Labor Union, the Socialist Trades and Labor Alliance, and the Industrial Workers of the World, all of them engaged in bitter and violent internecine warfare, as well as fighting the employers and the state.

In Canada, the two major union movements were the AFL and the Knights of Labor, both part of the Trades and Labour Congress of Canada until 1902. That year, on orders from Gompers, a resolution was passed expelling from the TLC the Knights of Labor and all other unions which did not belong to the AFL.

This was taken as an anti-French move because the Knights of Labor had been successful in recruiting unskilled workers — men, women, and children — from Quebec factories and mills, who were among the poorest and most exploited in the country. It was also a blow to Canadian unionism throughout the country, but this was countered by the belief that the AFL would supply the strength and solidarity to the struggling unions in Canada.

In 1891, a few years after its foundation, the Trades and Labour Congress presented its legislative program in a meeting with Sir John A. Macdonald, Canada's first prime minister, with the following demands: free, compulsory education; the eight-hour day; government inspection of all industries; public ownership of all public utilities; abolition of the Senate; abolition of child labour under fourteen years of age; abolition of property qualifications for all public bodies; and abolition of prison labour.[4]

Although this was limited legislation for a trade union body that claimed to speak for labour all over Canada, it nevertheless did show the Canadian labour movement as a force for progress. It also indicated that Macdonald, always the vote-getter, already recognized the potential of the labour movement in the Canadian body politic, even though he had no intention of granting any of the demands they had presented to him.

Of the three countries mentioned, Canada had undoubtedly the smallest labour movement as a percentage of the work force. During the period under review, the unions comprised 5 to 8 percent of a total work force that made up 37 percent of the population.[5]

Yet the advocacy in the TLC of a Canadian labour party was always heard, particularly at the annual conventions, although it was not until the convention of 1917, under the threat of conscription, and the break-up of the Liberal Party, that the first concrete measures were taken by the delegates to set up such a party. The outgoing executive council of the TLC recommended to the delegates the following action:

...we are of the opinion that the time has arrived when the workers of Canada should follow British precedent and organize a Labour Party upon such a basis that the trade unionists, socialists, fabiens [sic], co-operators and farmers can unite to promote legislation in the best interests of the wealth producers of the nation...With a view to giving effect to this recommendation we would strongly urge that the dominating working class political organization in each province call a conference of the respective organizations entitled to a partnership in such a Labour Party and proceed to co-operate for political action.[6]

The decision to field labour candidates by the Canadian Labour Party at this time turned out to be a mistake. The general elections took place within three months of the TLC convention, and labour was able to field only twenty-five candidates across the country, whose total vote was 37,500.[7]

The war was followed by unrest and upheavals in all countries that participated, most notably exemplified in the two revolutions of Russia in 1917, which effectively removed Russia from the war a year before its actual termination. In Canada this opened a new debate in the trade unions and their press, within the trade union federations and the TLC, and in the socialist parties, over which model should be followed — the British Labour Party or the Russian Bolshevik model.[8]

This debate was not confined to the labour movement. Such people as Mackenzie King, who was going to be a contestant for the leadership of the Liberal Party, the leaders of the Trades and Labour Congress, several leaders of the farmers movement, J. S. Woodsworth, and others, praised the manifesto of the British Labour Party, titled "Labour and the New Social Order," which among other things presented an outline for the welfare state. Professor R. M. MacIver, chairman of the Department of Political Economy, University of Toronto, in his book *Labor in the Changing World*, published April 1919, analyzed from a social-democratic viewpoint the changes brought about by the war: "Labor's horizon is no longer limited to the living wage. It has widened its claim. It demands a share in prosperity and a voice in control of industry." [9] Professor MacIver wrote this book as if he was answering Mackenzie King's earlier work *Industry and Humanity* with these words:

> Anyone who today speaks of the essential identity be-
> tween capital and labor is convicted thereby of either
> simplicity or hypocrisy.[10]

The executive council of the TLC directed its 1917 convention to begin preparations for participation in the general election as a labour party, and listed the organizations which would be eligible: "trade unionists, socialists, fabians, co-operators, and farmers..." There was no Fabian society in existence at that time, although Professor Mac-Iver did attempt to establish what he called the National Problems Club, but that never got off the ground.[11] The closest to a Fabian society was a group of Protestant ministers, centred in Winnipeg, clearly on the left and loosely called "practitioners of the social gospel." It consisted of Salem Bland, J. S. Woodsworth, William Irvine, and William Ivens.[12] They played an important role in bringing labour into political action as an independent force. It was not until 1932 before a group of academics founded the League for Social Reconstruction, and associated themselves with organizing social-democracy in Canada.[13] The chief factor in slowing down the formation of a Canadian labour party after the war was the split on this question in the trade union movement itself.

In September 1918, in Quebec City, two months before the war ended, the convention of the Trades and Labour Congress was torn apart by scenes of unprecedented turmoil, which ended with the western delegates deciding to hold a conference of their own, early in the new year. Although the main issue was the demand to change the structure of the movement from craft to industrial-type unionism, there were other pent up grievances which aggravated the delegates. At the Western Labour Conference, which convened in Calgary, March 1919, the demand for industrial unionism was adopted almost unanimously, but the delegates went much further and decided to call a constituent convention for June, in Winnipeg, to launch a new union movement called the One Big Union.

The Western Conference was led by prominent trade union leaders who were also members of the Socialist Party and the Social-Democratic Party. They introduced several resolutions in support of the new Bolshevik regime in Russia, which were passed unanimously.

In effect, the Conference had declared war on the Trades and Labour Congress and the American Federation of Labor, but had also severed its ties with the trade union movement from Ontario to the Maritimes. This was going to make it difficult if not impossible to carry on with the formation of the Canadian Labour Party, but most of the members of the socialist groups were now more interested in exploring the possibilities of setting up a political party with the Bolshevik Party as the model.

The most significant event of the labour movement at this time was the Winnipeg General Strike, which took place from May 15 until June 25, 1919. It was called by the Winnipeg Trades and Labour Council, the official body of the TLC and AFL, but the leaders of the strike, R. B. Russell and R. J. Johns, officers of the Metal Trades Council which had triggered the strike, were also leaders of the Socialist Party, as well as organizers of the forthcoming convention of the One Big Union, scheduled for June of the same year in Winnipeg. This put another obstacle on the path to a labour-backed political party.

The organized socialist movement, which had provided much of the leadership and initiative to the trade union movement, was now being diverted by the inauguration of the Communist International in Moscow, which appealed to socialists everywhere to abandon social democracy in favour of revolutionary socialism, now called "communism." The debate that began in 1919 and went on for almost two years was settled in 1921 in Canada, when some well known trade unionists joined the Communists even though they knew that this would mean complete submission to Moscow and the Comintern.[14]

The Western Conference proved to be a failure, because only a handful of trade unions, mostly from Winnipeg, broke away from the AFL to join the OBU. The Communist Party, on orders from Moscow, deserted the OBU and demanded that its members who were in the OBU withdraw as a condition of remaining in the party.

On the other side, there were some powerful advocates of a third party based on labour, among them J. S. Woodsworth, James Simpson, and William Irvine.

In the articles he wrote over an eighteen-month period, starting in August 1918, Woodsworth said at the outset:

> Now that the old parties have joined forces in a Union Government, it would seem that the democrats have a splendid opportunity to develop a genuine peoples' party in which farmers, industrial workers, returned soldiers, and progressives could all find a place.[15]

Immediately after the Winnipeg General Strike, Woodsworth looked upon the prospects for a third "peoples'" party with the same optimism:

> The strike is over. Its immediate ends have not been attained. But the workers have had a splendid training in economics and are united as never before. They may not all be perfectly clear as to just where they are going, but they know that they are on the way.[16]

Within a few months this optimism was given a boost by the Ontario elections of October 1919, with the triumph of forty-three candidates of the United Farmers of Ontario and twelve members of the Independent Labour Party, who joined together in a coalition to govern the province.

This victory was followed in quick succession by the election of eleven labour candidates in Manitoba in June 1920, and four in Alberta, where they were looked upon by the United Farmers of Alberta, which had become the government, as allies in the Legislature.

But the fact that only two of the labour candidates were elected in the December 1921 federal elections, was cause for concern in the labour movement.

The two people who had been elected on the labour ticket were J. S. Woodsworth in Winnipeg Centre, and William Irvine in Calgary East, both of whom had been Protestant ministers, completely dedicated to the service of labour. But what had happened to Ontario, where twelve prominent trade unionists were elected to the legislature as members of the Independent Labour Party just two years before?

For one thing, the divisions within and around the labour movement had become sharper. The Manitoba Independent Labour Party defied an appeal from the Winnipeg Trades and Labour Council to withdraw J. S. Woodsworth as a candidate in Winnipeg Centre in place of a candidate of the Canadian Labour Party. It had already rejected the CLP as a viable political instrument, which left the TLC and the Communists as the only affiliates of the CLP in Winnipeg, and the OBU and the ILP outside of it. Nevertheless, Woodsworth was elected, but R. B. Russell of the OBU, running on the Socialist Party ticket, was narrowly defeated in North Winnipeg by the Liberal lawyer who had defended the strike leaders. In other words, the federal election in Winnipeg after the General Strike, like the provincial election in Manitoba in 1920, reflected the continuing popularity there of the strike and everyone who had played a leading role in it.

But other issues had greater weight in various provinces. The ILP in Ontario supported the Winnipeg General Strike, although this never had the importance that it had in Winnipeg. The issues in the ILP began to turn on the growth of the United Farmers of Ontario, and the relations between it and the labour movement, which became crucial after the formation of a Farmer-Labour government. The ILP differed with the UFO on free trade, which the farmers considered to be the main plank in their federal platform, whereas the ILP stood for protectionism, which the Ontario labour movement considered crucial to its living standards. But since this was a federal jurisdiction, it did not play a big role on the provincial agenda, whereas the question of prohibition did, and caused irritation and at times conflict between the UFO and ILP. Within the UFO there was a growing feeling that its main ally should be the Liberal Party and not the ILP, and this sentiment grew over the years of the farmer-labour alliance under the slogan of "broadening out."

But the main division within the labour movement itself centred on the question of which political instrument it should foster: the Independent Labour Party, the Canadian Labour Party, or something else.

In Winnipeg, the choice according to Woodsworth was inevitable, if unfortunate:

> In the municipal elections of 1920 in Winnipeg, the bitter antagonism between the members of the American Federation of Labor and the One Big Union led to a split in the Dominion Labour Party. It was claimed that the Trades and Labour Council officials tried to dominate the political organization. The Independent Labour Party was formed by those who held that under existing conditions the political end of the movement must be entirely free, and membership open equally to Internationals or One Big Union.[17]

It is clear that in Winnipeg there would be no possibility of a serious labour party, which would exclude the OBU. Within a year the Canadian Labour Party in Winnipeg consisted of little more than the Trades and Labour Council and the Communists, whereas the Independent Labour Party had Woodsworth in the House of Commons, eleven members in the Manitoba Legislature, seven out of fourteen aldermen in the Winnipeg City Council, and all this was to be followed by the election of an ILP mayor, and another Member of Parliament, namely A. A. Heaps from North Winnipeg.[18]

The Canadian Labour Party in Ontario, however, had a different character and history, mainly because James Simpson, a former vice-president of the Trades and Labor Congress, and a long-time socialist, was convinced that this was the only path for labour to take, especially after he returned in February 1918 from the convention of the British Labour Party. The CLP would be, according to him, a federated party like the British one, and could bring together several groups and parties who would not agree on long-term fundamentals but could agree on a set of immediate reforms. In a practical sense this could have included the Independent Labour Party and the Communist Party.

Simpson, for most of the time that the CLP was functioning, had good relations with the Communists, who were elected to some important positions in it. At the CLP's 1924 convention, Woodsworth attended and participated in some of the events there, which he would not do in Manitoba. However, he did not accept any of the offices, honorary or otherwise, which the convention had offered him during the proceedings.

Yet the Communists were unable to work with Simpson, because of the changing demands made on them from Moscow. The Comintern had concluded that they were acting like social democrats when they should have been trying to isolate the leading social democrats in the CLP. Moreover, the Comintern had switched to a tactic of fighting the AFL, and this meant that the Canadian Communists were ordered to work with A. R. Mosher, of the Canadian Brotherhood of Railway Employees (CBRE), to form the All-Canadian Congress of Labour (ACCL) in November 1926, as one way of doing so. This was followed by the expulsion of Communist leader Jack MacDonald from the TLC for "dual unionism," a motion which was read at the convention of the TLC by James Simpson, who said:

> The Communist Party in this country is seeking to dictate not only the political policies of the working class, but the industrial policies as well.[19]

By the time this convention took place in September 1928, the Canadian Labour Party had disintegrated. It took ten years, from 1917 to 1927, to realize that the situation in the labour movement in Canada prevented all efforts to imitate the British Labour Party.

Yet it was becoming clear that the pattern and substance of politics in Canada had changed immeasurably after the war. It was clear that the two-party system was obsolete; but so was the Progressive Party, which had inspired hope of a successful third party. What could replace it?

Mackenzie King's book *Industry and Humanity* was published at the end of 1918. He also drafted a labour platform for the Liberal Party, which would be his banner going into the leadership convention in August 1919. He elaborated on these ideas during the general election in December 1921, from which he emerged as prime minister. He had borrowed much of his program from the post-war program of the British Labour Party: social insurance; unemployment insurance; workmen's compensation; health insurance; widows', maternity, and infant benefits; old age pensions; and a National Minimum Living Standard. He had become a liberal reformer, now at the head of the nation, with ideas that had never before surfaced in the House of Commons.

Social-democratic ideas certainly had been circulating in various ways, at least from the beginning of this century, if not before. An article in *The Canadian Magazine* in August 1894, entitled "Canadian Democracy and Socialism," explained:

> Karl Marx (1818–1883) is the author of the famous book: "Das Capital" — the Bible of social democrats and a book which has now great influence in the United States and Canada. He believed in evolution and that the present age of capitalistic production would pass away and be replaced by an association of laborers. To him in a great measure is due the International Working Men's Association, a society based on social democratic principles and intended to embrace all the laborers of Christiandom.[20]

Some of the other social-democratic books popular among Canadian socialists and radicals were J. A. Hobson: *Imperialism: A Study*; Phillips Thompson: *The Politics of Labor*; Edward Bellamy: *Looking Backward*; Gustavus Myers: *History of Canadian Wealth*, and numerous periodicals from the United States and Britain, as well as Canada. But because of the new situation in the western world after the war, and particularly after the Russian Revolution, a new definition or conception of social democratic thought was required. The Bolsheviks under Lenin had a different idea of socialism, which they contended was proven by their experience to be the only correct path for a Marxist revolution and a genuine socialist party.

In his series of essays in the *Western Labor News* from 1918–1919, Woodsworth revised his concept of socialism, taking into account the Russian and British experiences, but not at the expense of his analysis of the Canadian situation. He expressed it in Canadian terms: socialization of railways, telegraphs, mines, electric power, banks and insurance companies; the progressive socialization of large manufacturing and commercial institutions with compensation; and expropriation of unused land. In the social welfare field he proposed free health, medical and hospital services; free public education up to sixteen years of age; social insurance covering unemployment, sickness, and old age; good food, clothing, and shelter adequate for all; and housewives and mothers to be compensated by the state for their vital contribution to society.

These articles and the ideology which they projected would not have been as widely and effectively circulated but for his election to the House of Commons. In the twenty years that he was the member for Winnipeg North Centre, he made his program known. From his first speech in the House of Commons early in 1922, he explained these ideas with examples and statistics. He carried on a running battle for the abolition of the Senate; the amendment of the BNA Act to give the House of Commons the power to legislate on social measures; the repeal of the notorious Section 98 of the Criminal Code; the return of the RCMP to its constitutional role of policing the North-West Territories, and ending its surveillance of the labour movement and radical political parties.[21]

Woodsworth introduced a motion on April 10, 1922 to return the RCMP to its previous limited role. King had promised during the election campaign to do what Woodsworth now proposed, but he had changed his mind. The vote against the motion was 108 to 47, with all the Progressive members present, including their leader T. A. Crerar, supporting Woodsworth.[22]

In the first throne speech of the King government there was no mention of the sweeping reforms which had been King's election platform. Bruce Hutchison, in spite of his admiration for King as a small "l" liberal, explains it in this passage:

> In King's first Parliament the Welfare State was only a random arrow from Woodsworth's quiver. Industry and Humanity were still abstractions in King's mind, safely postponed. The great depression which would catalyze these things was still well hidden within the skyscrapers of Wall Street. The new society could wait.[23]

From the opening days of the King regime, and especially after Woodsworth's first speech, it gradually became evident that the centre of gravity in the House would be between King's liberalism and Woodsworth's socialism, and that the immediate target of each were the sixty-five MPs of the Progressive Party. By 1924, Woodsworth was the ideological leader of eleven Progressives, who, together with his colleague William Irvine, constituted what was called "the Ginger Group," and which by 1929 had grown to twenty-one.[24]

Among the agrarians in the Ginger Group at the outset, six were from Alberta, one each from Saskatchewan and Manitoba, and three from Ontario.[25] Mackenzie King, on the other hand, while emphasizing the importance of winning over all the Progressives to his side, directed most of his efforts at the Ontario Progressives, including those in the Ontario Legislature. He considered it a victory to have enticed Peter Heenan, one of the original twelve labour members in the Ontario Farmer-Labour government, to join the federal Liberal Party and become Minister of Labour. King made this comment on the Ontario Tory victory in 1923 over the Farmer-Labour government:

> ...now that the Tories are so strongly entrenched in power, and the evidence of the folly of divisions in the ranks of opposed forces so manifestly disclosed, I hope all our friends will see the political wisdom of doing their utmost to end divisions and bring about real union with the Progressives.[26]

The next two provincial elections in Ontario confirmed the decline in the political strength of the Progressives and the UFO although they held on to at least a dozen seats. A few labour men who had been active as ILP spokesmen, such as Peter Heenan and later Humphrey Mitchell, joined the Liberal Party and eventually became cabinet ministers. By the end of the 1920s, it appeared that Mackenzie King was making some headway in winning prominent labour leaders in Ontario to his ranks, but this did not translate into increased seats for the Liberals in Ontario until Hepburn's landslide victory in the provincial election of 1934, followed the next year by King's federal victory in Ontario, in which the Liberals won more seats than at any time since Confederation.

There were other issues and problems that had a bearing on labour unity, in particular on the question of independent labour political action. The problem of relations between English and French Canada, or more precisely of relations with Quebec, was a formidable obstacle.

The formation in 1921 of the Confédération des travailleurs catholiques du Canada (Canadian and Catholic Confederation of Labour) was announced by the Bishops of Quebec. From that time there were bitter conflicts between the Catholic unions and the Trades and Labour Congress in Quebec. Needless to say, this feuding at the trade union level would make it impossible for the two bodies to discuss seriously the creation of a political party of labour.

This relationship, or the lack of it, was in large measure due to the failure of English Canadians, including the left, to understand the national aspirations of French Canadians. There had been little, if any, co-operation during the war in the fight against conscription in English and French Canada, which weakened that fight considerably. The Farmer-Labour government of Ontario had promised to modify or repeal Regulation 17, enacted in 1912 under a Tory government, which eliminated French instruction in the province's schools. Premier E. C. Drury failed to live up to that promise, fearing a backlash from English voters.[27] He undoubtedly had the support on this question of the main trade unionists in Ontario.

J. S. Woodsworth too had difficulty in resolving the English-French dilemma, and could not understand why Quebec nationalists put so much emphasis on safeguarding their provincial rights. In the historic debate in Parliament in March 1927, he moved a resolution to enable the House of Commons to amend the BNA Act "while conserving the principles of confederation":

> I am not here to make any impassioned appeal to hon. members from the various sections of Canada. I know that in the past some of my French Canadian members have been rather apprehensive of any change in the British North America Act. I know that certain sections of the French Canadian press take the ground that any alteration

in the British North America Act might imperil French
Canadian rights and that it is much safer to trust to the
sense of justice of Englishmen in Great Britain than the
sense of justice of English-speaking Canadians. I think
that sentiment is unworthy of any true Canadian.[28]

Since the BNA Act had been a compromise to satisfy the Quebec
nationalists of that period, there could be no substantial amendment
to it without Dominion-Provincial agreement. Woodsworth, and the
dominant section of the English-speaking labour and socialist movements, wanted to change that, while guaranteeing "cultural rights" to
the French-Canadian "minority." This basically has been the position
of English-speaking social democracy in Canada ever since.

The ideological aspect of social-democratic thought in Canada
could be summarized from the speeches given in the House of Commons during the 1920s by the Ginger Group, but especially by Woodsworth, and his five articles on "Organizing Democracy in Canada"
in *The Western Labor News* from 1918 to 1919. They were anti-capitalist and anti-imperialist.

Woodsworth had been accepted by the entire Ginger Group as their
undisputed leader and it was his social-democratic vision of Canada
that acted as the catalyst in uniting its members. His aim was to form
a third party based on the interests of the farmers, workers, and small
businessmen. But the labour movement and the farmers' organizations, beset by internal divisions, were unable to unite politically, or
to resist the blandishments of Mackenzie King.

Woodsworth's vision of Canada was based on a strong central
government. He did not live to see another reality, that of provincial
governments of a social-democratic character, defending their provincial rights, and winning important social legislation on their
own, or as part of federal-provincial arrangements, as happened in
Saskatchewan.

4

The Third Party Revolt

The collapse of the third parties in the election of 1930 appeared
to write *finis* to the third party revolt that followed the war.

The Conservatives returned to power after an absence of almost
ten years, winning 49 percent of the votes and 137 seats, making this
its most impressive victory since Confederation. The Liberals, with
45 percent of the votes and 91 seats, became the official opposition,
and together the two main parties accounted for 228 seats and 94
percent of the popular vote. Nevertheless, there would be twelve
Progressives and with the addition of two new Labour members from
British Columbia, and the return of J. S. Woodsworth and A. A. Heaps
from Winnipeg, the Ginger Group totalled sixteen and would become
more cohesive in the next three years, under Woodsworth's leadership.

Yet this was a far cry from the massive bloc of sixty-five Progressives and two Labour members elected in 1921. Of the sixteen elected
in 1930, only one was from Ontario, which indicated that the efforts
to make the third party more than a western regional bloc had failed.
The majority of the twenty-four members from Ontario who had won
their seats as Progressives in 1921 had returned to the old parties,
mostly to the blandishments of Mackenzie King.

But Woodsworth had already decided that the time had come to
found the people's party which he had been advocating since 1919.
His first organizational steps were confined to the West in three
conferences to draft a program for a new national party: Regina in
1929, Medicine Hat in 1930, and Winnipeg in 1931.

With the depression spreading and deepening across the country,
he felt that it would be wrong to wait any longer. At the next confer-

ence, which was held in Calgary, August 1932, and attended by labour and socialist delegates from the West, farm representatives from the Prairie provinces, and the Ginger Group, a new party, called the Co-operative Commonwealth Federation (CCF), was launched with a mandate to call a founding convention for the following year in Regina, and to adopt a manifesto or program.

The major farm organizations, the United Farmers of Ontario, Alberta, Saskatchewan, and Manitoba, indicated that they would attend, but only a few trade unions had responded. A number of ILP branches would be represented, although only a few had any real success in elections, except in the municipal field. There was no indication that the small business men from the cities would attend, or that any effort had been made to involve them, even though Woodsworth in his articles had stressed the importance of the middle class as part of the new party.

A group of university professors from McGill and the University of Toronto had established the League for Social Reconstruction in March 1932, which from its outset was drawn towards the CCF.[1] In fact, two of its members, Frank Scott, professor of Law at McGill, and David Lewis, a student at McGill, became part of the national leadership of the CCF, and for the rest of their lives, were decisive in it and its successor, the New Democratic Party. Social democracy from that time on found an ever growing acceptance on English-Canadian campuses.

After the Calgary conference in 1932, which formally established the existence of the new party, J. S. Woodsworth and twelve other members of the House of Commons declared that henceforth they would call themselves CCF MPs.

In that capacity they launched a full-scale debate, commencing on February 1, 1933, by presenting to the House the following motion:

> Whereas under our present economic arrangement large numbers of our people are unemployed and without the means of earning a livelihood for themselves and their dependents;
>
> And whereas the prevalence of the present depression throughout the world indicates fundamental defects in the existing economic system;
>
> Therefore be it resolved: That, in the opinion of this House, the government should immediately take measures looking to the setting up of a cooperative commonwealth

in which all the natural resources and the socially necessary machinery of production will be used in the interests
of the people and not for the benefit of the few.[2]

The debate lasted intermittently over the entire month. The *Winnipeg Free Press* stated after the first week that it was "the major
event of the resumed session to date." [3] *The Canadian Forum* said
that it continued throughout the month to be "front page news," so
much so that Prime Minister R. B. Bennett and leader of the Opposition Mackenzie King made sure they were present every time Woodsworth was to participate.[4]

The debate was an historic moment in Canadian parliamentary
democracy. It was the first organized political response to the Great
Depression and mirrored the devastating conditions prevailing in the
country. Above all, the two main speeches were those of Woodsworth
and Mackenzie King, and not the prime minister, who failed to per-
ceive the nature of the depression or the significance of the birth of
the CCF, insinuating that this resolution originated in the Bolshevik
regime in Russia.

In introducing the resolution, Woodsworth said:

...this new organization is a federation rather than a party.
The farm bodies in the three western provinces and in
Ontario have already voted to affiliate. Further than that,
the political Labour bodies in the provinces from British
Columbia to Montreal have also voted to affiliate.

After dealing with some of the conditions in the country, he stated
that the real question was whether the changes that were urgent could
be brought about in a peaceable fashion or by other means. Did he
believe the wording of the resolution that the present Parliament or
any other capitalist parties that had a majority in the House would or
could implement the resolution? Or did he believe that it would
require a CCF majority in some future House before this would
happen?

Woodsworth recalled that a year previously (March 2, 1932) he
introduced a resolution which was almost identical to this one, except
that "there was no large body of organized opinion behind it. Today
that situation is altered, for last August there was organized the
Co-operative Commonwealth Federation." Mackenzie King waited
until February 27, at the end of the debate, and then delivered a

three-hour speech, which the *Winnipeg Free Press* characterized as "one of the major speeches of his political career." Faced with the founding of a party advocating a Canadian brand of socialism, and led by a credible spokesman, he spent most of that speech to prove that the immediate reforms in the platform of Woodsworth and the CCF could be carried out by the next Liberal government without bringing in socialism. Bruce Hutchison, in his book *The Incredible Canadian,* made this comment:

> His speech of that day was the first public proclamation that something decisive had occurred to him and his Party. It was, in fact, the outline of a new Liberal policy. Before his own leap leftward, King felt it necessary to demolish the CCF, his competitor for the leadership in reform.[5]

There were several important themes in Mackenzie King's speech, which were summed up in the following short paragraph:

> I think I have made clear, so far as the Liberal party is concerned, that we stand for many of the measures which might be included in a socialist program, and also that in so doing we are true to our past and our present, but that is vastly different from standing for a socialist state.[6]

As a corollary of that, he differentiated himself from the prime minister, R. B. Bennett, and his party, by saying that Woodsworth and the CCF were just as much opposed to communism and to violence as any other member of the House.

Another important theme in Mackenzie King's address was his assertion that Woodsworth and the other CCF MPs ignored the rights of the provinces as defined in the BNA Act:

> Is it conceivable that the various provincial administrations and the people in the different provinces will, at the instance of a new party that has been formed for less than a year, suddenly yield all their natural assets and the powers and rights they exercise as provinces over property and civil rights in order that a federal socialistic state may be formed in Canada? [7]

King concluded his address with a list of reforms that he would implement, and which he had written about in his *Industry and Humanity.*

By the time of the convention in July, the Regina Manifesto, which became the official program of the CCF, had been changed to incorporate some of the weaknesses which King had pounced on in the February debate in the House. The Manifesto added Clause 14, which contained "An Emergency Programme," to be carried out immediately by a CCF government, before tackling the socialist goals which would be of a fundamental nature. Section 9 was inserted, entitled "B.N.A. Act," which provided for the "amendment of the Canadian Constitution, without infringing upon racial or religious minority rights or upon legitimate provincial claims to autonomy, so as to give the Dominion government adequate powers to deal effectively with urgent economic problems which are essentially national in scope..."

This section expressed what has become a fundamental demand of CCF and NDP parties, regardless of the conditions prevailing at any time. They are dedicated to a strong centralized government in Ottawa wielding most of the powers, and with the powers of the provinces relegated to cultural and minority rights. Yet the CCF and its successor, the NDP, have never been close to federal power, but have been the government in four provinces, and have legislated to the benefit of the people there, and to the nation as a whole. The Saskatchewan CCF and NDP governments, for example, brought medicare to that province and forced the federal government and the other provinces to make it a shared-cost program.

During the debate on the co-operative commonwealth, Woodsworth emphasized that the political body that was coming into existence was not a party, but a federation, with the farm bodies of Ontario, Manitoba, Saskatchewan, and Alberta already affiliated, and many of the provincial labour bodies doing the same. But in the period following the Regina Convention, three of four farm bodies had disaffiliated, and after that, most of the labour groups, such as the Independent Labour Party, became branches of the CCF.

Frank Scott, in his article "The C.C.F. Convention" in *The Canadian Forum* of September 1933, praised the success of the convention: "On the whole, the Regina convention proved an outstanding success." Yet in that same article he said, "the Alberta and Ontario farmers were insistent upon their autonomy, and fought every attempt to restrict their independence. Clearly the issue is one which will have to be faced at future conventions." [8]

There were several issues that stood between the CCF and the farm bodies and probably the main one was the degree of socialism in the Regina Manifesto. The Manifesto committed the new federation to "socialization" of the economic order, of all financial machinery such as banking, currency, credit, and prices, of transportation, communications, and electric power, and all other industries essential to social planning. The members of the farm organizations found it difficult, and eventually impossible, to accept these points and one by one withdrew. The sections that were very strongly socialistic were taken almost word for word from the program that J. S. Woodsworth had published in 1919, and he insisted that they must be part of the program of the new party. Woodsworth emphasized that the new party must be a federation, but had regrets about it shortly after the convention. In a letter which he sent to members of the National Council on March 6, 1934, he complained that Communists had become part of the Ontario Labour Conference, which was affiliated to the CCF, and this made it "impossible to discipline them." In the same letter, discussing troubles between the UFO and the CCF, he wrote, "personally I think it was a mistake for the UFO to come in. It would have been better if we had from the first built an independent farmers' movement." [9]

In July 1934, at the convention of the United Farmers of Canada (Saskatchewan Section), it was decided that the political activities of the organization would be separated from their main body and these would be carried out by the "C.C.F. Saskatchewan Section." By the year 1939, all the affiliates of the CCF ceased to exist as such, and organizations such as the Socialist Party of Canada, Independent Labour Party, and Canadian Labour Party became regular branches of the CCF. Moreover, these branches were attached to provincial sections of the CCF, which became the basic legislative units of the national party, while still maintaining the misnomer of "Federation."

But with this program the CCF was confronted with serious obstacles in the provinces, especially in Ontario, Quebec, Alberta, and British Columbia.

Except for a small circle of academics at McGill around the League for Social Reconstruction, a few branches of socialist circles in the non-French community in Montreal, and some unions, particularly such needle trades unions as the International Ladies Garment Workers and the Amalgamated Clothing Workers, there were no CCF branches in Quebec at the time of the Calgary conference in 1932, or the founding convention in Regina in 1933. Yet the hierarchy of the

Roman Catholic Church in Quebec reacted quickly to these two events. In March 1933 it summoned the École sociale populaire to report on the Calgary program of the CCF and, in July 1933, to include the Regina Manifesto.[10]

The ESP inquiry, which was led by Père Georges-Henri Lévesque, rejected the CCF and its program as contrary to the doctrines of the Catholic Church, and presented an alternative thirteen-point "Programme for Social Restoration":

> Reform the capitalist system; develop the Christian spirit; moderate property rights; suppress the big monopolies; public ownership when it is for the public good; create an economic and social council; establish corporatism; introduce social-welfare; abolish unemployment, reduce hospital fees; aid to agriculture; strengthen provincial autonomy; respect between the two races.[11]

This program became the basis of an agreement between the Action Libérale nationale (ALN), a radical movement of young Liberals pressing in vain for sweeping changes in the provincial Liberal government, and the Conservative Party, which had just elected Maurice Duplessis as its Quebec leader, and appeared anxious and ready to accept any program which the young Liberals proposed. Under the banner of the Union nationale, this alliance swept into power in 1936, after which Duplessis expelled the ALN members from the cabinet, repudiated the joint program on which they had campaigned, and proceeded to put in place what would become the most reactionary and corrupt regime in Quebec's history.

The difficulties which the CCF had to face in Quebec were formidable, and the CCF national leadership was unable and unprepared to meet this challenge. The CCF developed out of conditions and movements that had taken place entirely in English Canada, mostly in the West, but also in Ontario, in the English-speaking communities in Montreal, and in some important segments of the Nova Scotia labour movement in Cape Breton. Very little effort was made to contact the francophones in Quebec or in the French-speaking regions of other parts of Canada. The role of some outstanding Protestant ministers was decisive in the foundation and program of the CCF, and this undoubtedly was a factor in their alienation from the French Canadians, who were Roman Catholic.

At the end of February 1934, Monsignor Georges Gauthier, Co-Adjutor Bishop of Montreal, issued a pastoral letter which banned Roman Catholics in that diocese from associating in any way with the new Co-operative Commonwealth Federation. The Archbishop stated that "no one can be at the same time a sincere Catholic and a true Socialist." Other accusations laid at the door of the CCF by the Archbishop were its demand for repeal of Section 98, by which the Communists had been ruled illegal; its proposals to amend the BNA Act to strengthen the federal powers, and to abolish the Senate; and its demand for federal legislation to improve working conditions, particularly those pertaining to young women and children.

No matter how many times J. S. Woodsworth answered these attacks, the Catholic hierarchy in Quebec did not lift the ban until October 1943. During that period, Premier Maurice Duplessis constantly slandered the CCF and threatened to use the infamous Padlock Law against its Quebec members.

On the other side, however, the CCF was isolated from most French Quebeckers by its unyielding position on the BNA Act. It stood for strengthening the federal powers at the expense of the provinces. Pierre Trudeau, who favored some aspects of the CCF-NDP, explained in a 1961 article that he could not join because of its attitude to French Canada:

> ...the CCF has reaped little electoral reward for its studied application in speaking with one voice and acting with one purpose in all parts of Canada. In Quebec alone, where the socialist vote has usually hovered around one per cent of the total, a book could be filled with the frustrations of former members of the CCF who felt or imagined that provincial affairs must always be subordinate to the *raison d'Etat* of the national party.[12]

All the provincial governments at the beginning of the depression were turned out of office during the ten years that it lasted. The Liberal Party of British Columbia defeated the Conservatives in 1933 with a New Deal platform, a slogan "Work and Wages," and a promise of a new social order. The newly formed CCF, just a month after the Regina Convention, elected seven members to the British Columbia Legislature, with 32 percent of the popular vote, and became the official opposition. This would continue the tradition in which there had been socialists in every British Columbia Legislature from the turn of the century.

The CCF in Saskatchewan, contesting its first provincial election in 1934, won 25 percent of the vote and five seats to become the official opposition. David Smith, a political scientist at the University of Saskatchewan, has made this judgement:

> ...The formation and growth of the new party, first as the Farmer-Labor Party,and then as the Co-operative Commonwealth Federation, was the most significant feature of Saskatchewan politics during the decade of depression and drought.[13]

However, the CCF in Ontario was at a standstill during the depression. There was turmoil in the Ontario Labour Conference over the admission of Communists, and Woodsworth, in a sudden and surprising move, retaliated by lifting Ontario's charter. Within a year after the 1933 convention, the United Farmers of Ontario withdrew from the CCF, and when the provincial election was called for June 19, 1934, the CCF was not prepared.

The Ontario Liberals, who had not been in office since 1905, entered this election with a new and ebullient leader, Mitchell Hepburn, a farmer who had decided to campaign for sweeping reforms, as he explained in a public meeting in May, 1932:

> I favour calling all the leaders together, Liberal, Progressive, and Labour. I would have us discuss our common interests and see along the same lines. Let me repeat that I swing well to the left, where even some Liberals will not follow me, but if it's necessary for me to travel alone, I will. I hope to see a complete realignment of thought in this country.[14]

In this campaign he became a strong admirer of Franklin D. Roosevelt's "New Deal" and promised to use the same methods to alleviate the conditions of the people of Ontario. He targeted the labour vote and attacked the anti-labour record of the Conservative regime. The Liberals won seventy seats, plus two Progressives who would be working with them; the Conservatives, who had been the government of Ontario since 1923, kept only seventeen seats; and the CCF, running for the first time, elected one.

The CCF did get 109,000 votes, or 7 percent of the total, but it was the Liberals who won the labour vote, as demonstrated in the industrial ridings, and this would be repeated in Ontario in the federal elections a year later.

But the biggest blow the CCF received was the emergence and victory of the Social Credit League in Alberta in the provincial election of August 22, 1935, and the federal election of October 14. They were at the expense of the prevailing government, the United Farmers of Alberta, which had affiliated to the CCF at the founding convention. In *The Canadian Forum* of February 1934, Elmer E. Roper, the leader of the Alberta CCF, expressed unwavering confidence that the alliance of the CCF and UFA would win the next provincial and federal elections in that province. Instead, Social Credit, which was not yet formed in 1934, won fifty-seven of the sixty-three seats in the Legislature, fifteen of seventeen seats in the House of Commons from Alberta, and two in Saskatchewan.

The theory or idea of social credit originated in Britain shortly after the First World War out of several books by an engineer, Major C. H. Douglas. His thesis was that the total sum of wages and salaries is always less than the price of the goods produced, and if this imbalance is not corrected, periodic slowdowns will occur and eventually the economy will collapse. The needed correction must be the infusion of added purchasing power by the state through its ability to issue some form of social credit.

The first important indication in Canada of "the Douglas system," came on June 5, 1922, in the speech on the federal budget by William Irvine, who had been elected to the House of Commons from Calgary East as a Labour member, and who was a close colleague of J. S. Woodsworth, the other Labour member in the House. Irvine spoke of the Douglas system, "which I do not contend is the only possible way … but … there are in connection with this system certain fundamental principles which I claim to be undeniable …"[15]

Irvine visited Douglas that same year in England, and was instrumental in having him invited to appear in 1923 before the House Standing Committee on Banking and Commerce. He arranged for the United Farmers of Alberta to print some articles by Douglas in the UFA magazine in the early 1930s. William Aberhart, principal of a Calgary high school and a lay preacher of the Calgary Prophetic Bible Institute, who was also conducting a weekly radio talk, began to introduce his own interpretation of Douglas's ideas on social credit to his growing and receptive radio audience. Aberhart challenged the

UFA government to implement social credit by issuing monthly dividends of $20 or $25 to every adult in Alberta. From that point on, the momentum for social credit was sweeping the province, but the UFA leaders declared that they had been unable to get a satisfactory explanation from either Major Douglas or William Aberhart on how they would operate the system in one province, when the provinces did not have the constitutional jurisdiction over banking, credit, or currency. Aberhart then announced the formation of the Social Credit League, and the provincial elections, which took place only a few months later, ended in a great victory for the Social Credit, an unbelievable disaster for the farmers' own party, which had been in power since 1921.

The federal election of October 14, 1935 compounded the situation: the CCF, making its first appearance as a federal party, contested fifteen of the seventeen federal ridings in Alberta, and elected none, whereas the Social Credit League, contesting all seventeen seats, elected fifteen. William Irvine, so prominent in the UFA, and as a Labour MP from Alberta from 1921 to 1935, except for one year, and the person who was the first to popularize "the Douglas system" in Canada, fell victim to its popularity, and that of its latter day advocates.

The CCF, in its Regina Manifesto, had stated its position on social credit, which in fact was very similar to the 1919 program of Woodsworth:

2. SOCIALIZATION OF FINANCE

Socialization of all financial machinery — banking, currency, credit, and insurance, to make possible the effective control of currency, credit and prices, and the supplying of new productive equipment for socially desirable purposes.

Therefore, the CCF would not impose the social credit solution unless it was elected to run the federal government. No province has the constitutional right to issue money or certificates, which in fact would mean printing money. When it became clear to the people of Alberta that the provincial government did not have the powers to implement any part of the social credit legislation, they blamed it on Mackenzie King and the banks, and applauded Aberhart when he wrote to King and said: "... May I issue a most solemn warning to you and the Banks that our people have tightened their belts to the limit, and if you and the Banks are allowed to continue with the policy that you have been carrying out for years, it will mean starvation of our people ... for the sake of OUR PEOPLE we are compelled to carry on in the face of all opposition." [16]

With this kind of rhetoric, Aberhart inherited Alberta's populism, which from 1921 had expressed itself through successive UFA governments against the Liberals and Conservatives. The people now found in the Social Credit League a rejuvenated fighter against what the earlier farmers' movements had called the "Triple Alliance" of banks, railways, and big monopolies. The CCF, which had just recently come into existence as a party, united in its ranks people who had also been opposed to the triple alliance, but the CCF was identified with the UFA, which had become lethargic, and tainted with scandal. The CCF was also identified with socialism which Aberhart told the people was unnecessary to bring about a universal rise in their purchasing power.

Yet another party came into existence in the months prior to the 1935 federal elections. The Reconstruction Party was led by Harry H. Stevens, a maverick Conservative, who had been a cabinet minister for most of Bennett's regime but resigned or was fired over policy differences. But R. H. Wilbur wrote in his biography of Stevens, "the Reconstruction party was largely an act of political desperation; it had no ideological base to compare with that of the CCF or even the Social Credit ..." [17] This party did capture attention for a brief moment of history, but it died after the election.

The year 1935 was in many respects a watershed politically, and to a lesser but significant extent, economically. It began with seven broadcasts by Prime Minister R. B. Bennett:

> In the first days of 1935, the Canadian people could not believe their radios. From the winter silence boomed the familiar voice of the Prime Minister announcing that society must be overhauled from top to bottom and that he would overhaul it. There would be a New Deal for everybody ... [18]

Bennett was the latest and most unlikely Canadian politician to climb aboard U.S. President Franklin D. Roosevelt's popular New Deal. He presented his New Deal to Parliament in the form of legislative enactments limiting working hours, establishing minimum wages, setting up unemployment insurance, controlling marketing and pricing of certain basic materials, and providing for relief of farm debtors, all of which were declared, a year later, by the Judicial Committee of the House of Lords in London, to be *ultra vires*.[19]

Even while Bennett was debating his New Deal legislation, thousands of unemployed single men poured out of "slave labour camps," and declared that they were heading for Ottawa on the freight cars of the CNR and CPR to protest the conditions to which they were subjected. This movement touched the conscience of Canada. Here before the eyes of the nation were the representatives of a whole generation of Canada's youth, abandoned by the system, and ignored by the governments.

Bennett, still unable to show any compassion for the plight of these unemployed men, played out to the very end the idea that this was a "Communist plot." Bennett decided to end the protest at Regina. The result was a brutal police attack on the men and their supporters, with one constable dead and close to a hundred police and demonstrators hospitalized. This dealt a fatal blow to the already discredited regime of R. B. Bennett.[20]

The election was a victory for the Liberal Party of Mackenzie King, which took 173 of 245 seats, his best win by far since he first ran as leader in 1921. He finally broke through in Ontario with 56 seats out of 82, as contrasted with the previous results there: 1921 — 21 seats, 1925 — 11, 1926 — 26, and 1930 — 22. He could say that, at last, he was recognized in Canada's leading industrial province as an expert in labour relations, and a friend of the working man. This was due to a number of factors, but the resentment against the anti-labour policies of the Bennett regime was probably the main reason. Labour voted against Bennett and for King, who was perceived as the only alternative.

There were three other parties running in a federal election for the first time. The CCF was actually established as a party in August 1932; the Social Credit and the Reconstruction Party both appeared in 1935, shortly before the election was called.

The CCF fielded 118 candidates, who received a total of 387,056 votes, but elected only 17. Social Credit ran 45 candidates, with a vote of 180,301, and elected 7. But the situation with the Reconstruction Party was the most lopsided: it ran 174, received about the same number of votes as the CCF, but elected only its leader.

The Reconstruction Party provided an alternative for dissident Conservatives. Its votes were mostly in the larger cities of central and eastern Canada, among anglophones of lower and middle class, who saw their savings and property disappearing. This party dissolved immediately after the election.

The CCF won only seven seats — three in British Columbia, and two each in Saskatchewan and Manitoba. The defeat in Alberta was a bad blow, because the UFA, which was now part of the CCF, had nine seats in the previous House of Commons.

The Communist Party of Canada, which was founded as the Workers' Party in 1922, entered the election of 1935 with a different outlook than it had in previous federal and provincial elections. With the rise to power of Hitler and Mussolini, the Communist International adopted the tactic known as the "popular front," whereby the Communists in democratic countries would now take seriously the defence of "bourgeois democracy" and seek to unite with liberals and social democrats against right-wing politicians, who it was presumed were fascists or semi-fascists. Tim Buck, the leader of the Canadian Communists, had become well known as a result of being imprisoned in Kingston Penitentiary where he was shot at by a prison guard. The CPC nominated him in North Winnipeg, where he would have to defeat the sitting member, A. A. Heaps of the CCF, in spite of the fact that this would violate the party's appeal to the CCF for a united front. Buck did not win, but he received 7,300 votes, a record for a Communist up to that point. J. B. McLachlan, the leader of the Mine Workers Union in Cape Breton, received 5,365 votes on the Communist ticket. Altogether the Communists ran thirteen candidates in six provinces and received a total of 32,000 votes. These were, of course, in Communist strongholds, but the time was not ripe for Communists to win provincial and federal elections, although they had begun to win seats in municipal councils and school boards.[21]

Within weeks of his inauguration as president of the United States in 1933, Franklin D. Roosevelt drafted a series of legislative enactments, which he called the New Deal. These would change the social conditions in that country and, for the first time in this century, bring about mass movements *in support* of an American president. There is no doubt that the impact of the New Deal spilled over into Canada, although some of the politicians who sought to be identified with it had no intention of carrying out such a radical program.

At the start of the depression in the United States conditions were worse than in Canada. The protest movements that were already in existence, such as populist, socialist, communist, radical, labour, and reformist, began to grow again. But within two years after the launching of the New Deal, Roosevelt pre-empted them all, and became the spokesman for the centre and the left of centre. This was particularly evident in what happened to the Socialist Party of America. Its leader and candidate for president, Norman Thomas, received 900,000 votes in 1932 and 200,000 in 1936. Prominent leaders in the trade unions, who had supported him in 1932, resigned from the Socialist Party to openly campaign for Roosevelt in 1936.[22] This did not happen in Canada, at least not to that extent. There is no doubt that the Liberal leaders in B.C. and Ontario became New Dealers at least for the duration of their election campaigns, but the spectacle of R. B. Bennett climbing on the New Deal wagon could not convince the voters that he had been converted. Mackenzie King did not endorse or appear to be a supporter of the New Deal, lest he would have to deliver specific reforms if he was returned to office. Woodsworth remained consistent with his platform; while it contained immediate reforms, it adhered to the Regina Manifesto, which pledged the CCF to "eradicate capitalism." As the depression continued and deepened, he was more than ever convinced that socialism was the only solution to the depression, and that any praise for the New Deal by him would confuse the issue.

The most specific aspect of the New Deal to affect Canada, was the Committee for Industrial Organization (CIO), which was established by the AFL, but later expelled from the AFL to become the Congress of Industrial Organizations, headed by John L. Lewis. The CIO organized millions of industrial workers in the major industries of the USA, but the impetus for this great growth of trade unionism was clearly the passage in 1935 by the President and Congress of a New Deal bill, popularly called the Wagner Act, which became a virtual charter of working-class rights. It guaranteed the right of collective bargaining and outlawed the so-called "company unions" for the first time in U.S. history.

The massive drives which the CIO undertook in auto, steel, electrical, chemical, and rubber industries were highly successful. Workers appealed to the new union movement to come in and help them organize. The CIO entered the strike of the auto workers at General Motors in Oshawa in 1937 and in spite of the attempts by Premier Hepburn to keep the CIO out of Ontario, General Motors eventually recognized the United Auto Workers of the CIO as the bargaining unit for their workers in Oshawa.

This was followed by an upsurge in "organizing the unorganized" in Canada under the CIO, especially in Ontario, in steel, electrical, packinghouse, rubber, chemical, and metal mining industries. Hepburn fought these unions, especially the metal miners, who waged bitter strikes in 1940 in Sudbury and Kirkland Lake, in which Hepburn openly sided with the mine owners, many of whom were his personal friends.

In Quebec, Premier Maurice Duplessis launched a similar attempt to smash the CIO, but his attack was also directed at the militant section of the Catholic unions, which had carried out prolonged and bitter strikes.[23] The anti-labour stances of the governments of Ontario and Quebec were so similar that they earned the epithet, "the Duplessis-Hepburn Axis."

The organizing drives were impeded by the attacks of Duplessis and Hepburn. There were no labour codes such as the Wagner Act anywhere in Canada until February 1944, when Mackenzie King, under mounting pressure from the trade unions, passed order-in-council PC 1003, which afforded trade unions the same protection as the U.S. workers had for over eight years under the Wagner Act.

The trade union membership in Canada grew rapidly between 1936, when it was 323,000, and the end of the war in 1945, when it reached 711,000. In other words, from the time the trade unions in Canada began in earnest to "organize the unorganized," membership doubled in less than ten years. This slogan had been foremost at the Western Labour Conference in Calgary, 1919. The movement which was projected then, with the visionary title, One Big Union (OBU), did not materialize at that time, but in a way the coming of the CIO, based on industrial unions, was the embodiment of this earlier vision.

But the growth of the trade union movement in this period did not result immediately in a growth of labour political action. In fact it had the opposite effect. In the United States, the AFL under William Green fought the expansion of the CIO and forced its expulsion. This created two trade union centres, and intra-union conflict. The AFL ordered the Trades and Labour Congress of Canada to expel all CIO unions from its ranks. The latter then joined with the All-Canadian Congress of Labour, which up to that time was made up of unions who had been barred from the TLC because they were Canadian. The result was the formation of the Canadian Congress of Labour (CCL), with mixed affiliations, but with the majority of the membership in CIO unions in Canada.[24]

The formation of the CCL, and the continued expansion of industrial unions under the CIO, ushered in a period of battles between the Communist Party (later called the Labor-Progressive Party) and the CCF over the issue of labour political action. The CCF wanted

the unions to affiliate to it for political action; the Communist Party
and the Liberals united to try to prevent the CCF from succeeding.[25]
This battle went on for several years, but by 1943, with a big labour
sweep to the CCF in Ontario, it seemed that the CCF had at last
become the working-class party in industrial Ontario.

Prior to this, various attempts were made by the Communist Party
to win members of the CCF to a "united front" or "popular front" to
fight fascism. But the Communists made sure that their appeals to the
CCF on these issues were directed only to the "left" or "centre-left"
members, by denouncing at every stage the leaders, such as Woodsworth, Heaps, Coldwell, MacInnis, and Lewis, and labelling them
"right-wing." When the battle erupted within the Canadian CIO, the
Communists classified almost every CCF trade union official in the
CIO as an "enemy."

Quite apart from the trade union battles, the Communists in Alberta
formed alliances with the Social Credit, even with Aberhart, in their
attempts to isolate the CCF.[26]

The CCF in the 1930s spent a great deal of time fighting the
Communist Party. The minutes of the CCF National Council and
Executive Committee are replete with references to various actions
taken by the Communists, which were considered to be harmful to
the CCF, and counter measures that were taken, such as the sudden
action of J. S. Woodsworth in March 1934, in removing the charter
of the Ontario Provincial Council for allowing Communists to join
the CCF. He had never before taken such a determined, and what
some CCFers thought arbitrary, action. The time spent on fighting the
Communists was at the expense of more important work, but Woodsworth believed that any link with the Communists would do irrepa-
rable harm to the CCF. In an article in 1936, he explained in some
detail why he took that position:

> In Canada, a linking of the CCF with the Communist Party
> involves, in my judgement, the destruction of the
> CCF...Under a united front the Communist Party might
> stand to gain. The CCF would be split from stem to stern,
> and the people's mass movement set back for decades.[27]

He was also opposed to links with the Social Credit, the Liberals,
and the short-lived New Democracy, which was a federal extension
of Social Credit. After the election of 1935 he severely reprimanded
T. C. Douglas for accepting help in his election campaign from the

Social Credit in his riding, and later, because he allowed his name to appear on the letterhead of the League Against War and Fascism, a Communist-sponsored "united front" organization.

Woodsworth's position on this question was upheld at the 1936 convention by a vote of eighty-eight to seven. It was explained in the September edition of *The Canadian Forum* by David Lewis:

> A fusion of the CCF, Communists, Social Crediters, Re-constructionists, and Left Liberals, — which is what the Communists advocate, — would, under present Canadian conditions, create confusion, compromise the socialist ob-jective and the CCF as a party, and might even, by way of reaction, call forth a strengthening of the right forces.[28]

The determination of the CCFers to stay clear of alliances was mainly rooted in the fear of too close association with Mackenzie King. In the 1920s, King on several occasions invited Woodsworth and Heaps into his cabinet. In his famous speech of February 27, 1933, he attempted to head off the establishment of the CCF by suggesting that it could work together with him and the Liberal Party to bring about much needed reforms to improve the conditions of the people, without socialism.

Woodsworth had strong objections to co-operating with the Liber-als: the CCF must keep socialism uppermost in its program, and in strong centralized government, whereas King adhered to the federal-provincial system which leaves social legislation to the provinces.

In spite of the CCF program, which stressed its national aspects, the development of the party was taking place at the provincial level, and this was producing centrifugal aberrations which were causing concern in the Executive Council. Frank Underhill, in an article in *The Canadian Forum* of August 1936, denounced this tendency:

> The 1933 Regina convention gave it a platform in the Regina Manifesto which has abundantly justified itself in the last three years as a unifying agency. But since then it has tended to disintegrate into little provincial parties, each running its own show without much attention to the national field. *If such tendencies develop further they will be fatal to the movement as a whole, since the vital ele-ments in the socialist programme depend upon national action.*[29]

But that tendency did not abate, because the main victories that the CCF and its successor, the NDP, achieved throughout its history, were at the provincial level, even though the centralist aspects of the provincial platforms they adopted, remained.

The decade of the depression changed the political party system. The CCF and the Social Credit emerged as two new parties functioning at the federal and provincial level; and the Union nationale in Quebec. In spite of this, however, the two major parties survived and remained the major federal parties. From the viewpoint of policies, there were no fundamental changes until the end of the 1939-1945 war. But the changes in Canadian society that did take place then were the results of the turmoil and discontent of the Thirties, and the impact of the newly-formed and social-democratic CCF.

The rigid determination of the CCF not to budge in any way from its stand on centralized government was reinforced in two publications: the League for Social Reconstruction's *Social Planning For Canada*, a 524-page volume on political economy published in 1935, and a pamphlet, *Canada — One or Nine?*, which was its submission in 1938 to the Royal Commission on Dominion-Provincial Relations. In both, the LSR reiterated its interpretation of the BNA Act of 1867, and added two changes necessitated by the depression: the Dominion Parliament must be given the right to provide social services and a basic minimum standard of living to everyone in Canada and the right to control and direct long-range economic planning. "To maintain and carry out these purposes, the Dominion Parliament must be restored to its former position of authority over all matters of national importance affecting the welfare of Canadians in all the provinces." [30]

The CCF and its "brain trust," the LSR, prescribed the same measures for correcting the BNA Act in a socialist society, as well as for an emergency such as a capitalist depression. In the meantime, the developments that were taking place in the United States under Roosevelt indicated that there were still measures available which could alleviate the hardships and improve the economy, even if the capitalists resisted most of the reforms of the New Deal. Upton Sinclair, the renowned American writer of that period, expressed it this way:

> Under President Roosevelt's leadership, the Democratic party is rapidly becoming a left wing party. President Roosevelt has talked more to the left than he has acted, but talk by a president in this country is action, and as a

result Roosevelt has earned the bitter hatred of the exploit-
ing classes, and they are making against him what is
becoming more and more clearly a straight class fight. The
rich are against him, while the poor and the unemployed
are for him.[31]

It can be said, however, that the successes of Roosevelt's New
Deal spilled over into Canada, especially in Canadian labour. But the
two parties that might have benefited from becoming associated in
the public's image with the New Deal — the CCF and the Liberals
— for their own reasons shunned such an identity.

5

The CCF and the War Against Fascism

...we believe that genuine international co-operation is incompatible with the capitalist regime which is in force in most countries, and that strenuous efforts are needed to rescue the League of Nations from its present conditions of being mainly a League of capitalist Great Powers. We stand resolutely against all participation in imperialist wars...Canada must refuse to be entangled in any more wars fought to make the world safe for capitalism.
— From Article 10, Regina Manifesto, adopted by the CCF at its first convention, July 1933.

When that clause was adopted, Hitler had been in power for only six months, and the Soviet Union had not yet joined the League of Nations. When the war started in September 1939, Hitler had conquered the Ruhr Valley, Austria, and Czechoslovakia. Together with Mussolini of Italy, he had defeated the legal and democratic government of Spain and had installed Generalissimo Francisco Franco as dictator. Internally, Hitler had begun the massacre of Jews, and the imprisonment of thousands of people who had opposed him before 1933. Mussolini had invaded Ethiopia, and Japan, a new partner, had invaded China. A few weeks prior to the declaration of war, Hitler scored a major triumph by signing a Non-Aggression Pact with Stalin, which cleared the way for a war against Britain and France.

These events made the CCF's "External Relations" clause in the Regina Manifesto obsolete. David Lewis, in his memoirs, recalled the debates that occurred in the CCF and in its parliamentary caucus as it became clear that it was not only a clash between rival imperialist powers, but also between democracy and fascism, and against the brutal racism of the Nazi philosophy.[1] CCFers differed in their interpretation of these events. Pacifists and doctrinaire socialists tended to support Woodsworth, but a growing number believed that Hitlerism was more than the ordinary imperialist enemy and would have to be defeated militarily.[2]

Yet when Hitler invaded Poland on September 1, 1939, followed by declarations of war by Britain and France, and the Canadian Parliament was summoned into special session on September 8 to do the same, the CCF was unprepared to take a stand much beyond the Regina Manifesto.

At a hurried emergency meeting of the CCF National Council convened on September 6, it became clear that Woodsworth would not agree to any formulation except the one in the Manifesto. It was decided that he would present his own ideas in the House of Commons and M. J. Coldwell would state the majority view of the National Council. But in spite of David Lewis's assertion that the two declarations were different, there was, in fact, little to distinguish between them.

Woodsworth, in his speech in Parliament, admitted that there were differences between Great Britain and Hitler's Germany, but these were insufficient to justify Canadian participation in the war alongside Britain. He concluded his statement, which was unusually emotional for Woodsworth, with these words:

> We laud the courage of those who go to the front; yes, I have boys of my own, and I hope they are not cowards, but if any of those boys, not from cowardice but really through belief, is willing to take his stand on this matter and, if necessary, to face a concentration camp or a firing squad, I shall be more proud of that boy than if he enlisted for the war.[3]

M. J. Coldwell then presented the official position of the majority of his party's National Council. He agreed that there were some exceptional differences between this war and the War of 1914 to 1918; that

> ... Canada is now implicated in a struggle which may
> involve the survival of democratic institutions ... and the
> people of Britain and France are waging a war against
> aggression ... In view of these considerations, the CCF
> believes that Canada's policy should be based first on the
> fundamental national interests of the Canadian people, as
> well as on their interest in the outcome of the war. Canada
> should be prepared to defend her own shores, but her
> assistance overseas should be limited to economic aid and
> must not include conscription of man power or the sending
> of any expeditionary force.[4]

Given its best interpretation, Coldwell's statement was lukewarm,
and its opposition to "the sending of any expeditionary force"
nullified whatever he had to say about supporting Canadian participation in the war against Hitler. The arguments that Woodsworth and
Coldwell utilized, in addition to those in the Manifesto, had to do with
their distaste for the policy of "appeasement" pursued by Neville
Chamberlain, prime minister of Britain, and Edouard Daladier
premier of France, by which they had given in to Hitler's demands
up to then, and therefore had helped bring about the war. Many CCF
MPs attacked Mackenzie King's opposition to sanctions against
Italy's invasion of Ethiopia, although Woodsworth supported King.
Most of the members opposed the non-intervention fiasco which cut
off supplies to the legal and democratic government of Spain, while
Hitler and Mussolini were supplying arms, aircraft, pilots, and officers to the Franco fascists. Although critical of King's policies, the
CCF was not prepared to endorse his measures for Canada's war
effort, not even a telegram from Arthur Greenwood, acting leader of
the British Labour Party, which stated:

> ...the common peoples of many lands have been hurled
> into cruel conflict by Hitler in furtherance of his ambitious
> aims at domination and conquest; his responsibility is
> criminal, his excuse a lie. With firm resolution and without
> passion we have accepted his brutal challenge, we are
> animated by a single and steadfast purpose...[5]

According to David Lewis, it took three years before the CCF had
come to a full realization of the anti-fascist character of the war, and

therefore would be prepared to support it fully. The CCF began to change perceptibly, as he put it, within a year

> ... as Hitler simply walked through Denmark and Norway in April 1940 and Holland and Belgium the following month. We gasped in disbelief when the Nazis easily conquered France in June and succeeded in setting up a collaborationist government under General Petain...by the summer of 1940, Britain stood alone against Hitler in Europe. And in Britain itself there had been a dramatic change in government; Churchill replaced Chamberlain as prime minister and the Labour Party joined his cabinet in some of the crucial posts ... in June 1941 when Hitler attacked the USSR ... and in December when Japan descended on Pearl Harbour and the USA entered the war. By 1942 the CCF was totally committed.[6]

There is no doubt that this hesitancy cost the CCF some of its support. In the snap election called by Mackenzie King for March 1940, the CCF polled the same vote it had received in 1935: 393,230 or 8.5 percent of the total votes cast. It elected eight candidates against its previous seven, but considering that this was the second time it participated in a federal election, it was a disappointment. A. A. Heaps, who had been the member for North Winnipeg through four successful campaigns, was defeated this time, undoubtedly due to losing a large number of Jewish voters who wanted more than a lukewarm response to the war against Hitler. Heaps's biography, written by his son Leo, claims: "The Jewish electors of North Winnipeg pledged mass support for the Liberal, Lieut. Col. C. S. Booth as the candidate most likely to further the war effort. No matter what Heaps said, the opposition did everything to brand him, in a riding with strong European ties, as a pacifist."[7] On the other hand, Woodsworth in the next constituency was returned, but by the narrow margin of 125 votes, as compared with the 1935 election when his margin over his nearest rival was 4,000 votes.

After the opposition to the war subsided in the CCF, and a majority was convinced that it was a just war, the party had to set out new priorities, which consisted of defending trade union rights in a wartime economy, and civil rights in view of the promulgation of the War Measures Act. It had to decide what stand to take on the national referendum on conscription; and it felt compelled to project the kind of life in post-war Canada that would make the sacrifices of the war worthwhile.

On the War Measures Act, the CCF caucus led by M. J. Coldwell took the position that "in wartime every Government must have the power to detain persons trying to commit acts against the interests of the State," and therefore it supported the inclusion in the Defence of Canada Regulations of Section 21, which authorized the Minister of Justice to detain people without trial for unspecified periods "at his discretion." On April 1, 1941, Coldwell met a delegation of the families of Communists who were interned under this clause, and said that in their cases he believed that the interned men should be tried in court if there was any evidence of subversive activities, and if not, they should be released. In the meantime, he thought that the review board which consisted of one person should be increased to three.[8]

The CCF did not participate in Parliament in the debate in 1942 on the removal of Japanese Canadians from their homes in British Columbia and their expulsion into other provinces in concentration camps or similar dwellings. But at the B.C. CCF provincial convention the following year the party endorsed the evacuation, and advocated that the Japanese Canadians should not be allowed to take up residence in the coastal areas after the war.

On the plebiscite on conscription, the National Executive, meeting on March 21-22, 1942, accepted with little enthusiasm a resolution which said that inasmuch as "the plebiscite is being held...it should be answered by a "Yes" vote.[9]

At the CCF's Seventh National Convention, held in Toronto, July 1942, the delegates adopted a utopian program, titled "For Victory and Reconstruction," which proclaimed that "we must make it clear that the present struggle against international Fascism is part of the people's revolution to usher in a new era of brotherhood and security for all the peoples of the world." [10]

But the CCF found itself in a number of battles inside and outside the House of Commons and the Legislatures on all these issues. The most immediate were those taking place in the trade unions, particularly in the growth of the CIO in Canada, and the attempt of governments to compel the workers to shoulder a disproportionate share of the wartime sacrifices.

To the applause of the employers, the King government imposed overtime work without overtime rates; wage controls; refused to enact equal pay for women, who then were entering the work force to replace the men who had joined the armed services; compulsory cooling-off periods in labour-management negotiations. At the same time the government rejected labour's demand for a labour code which would protect by law the rights of unions to organize and bargain collectively, as the U.S. Wagner Act did in the United States.

With the extraordinary proliferation of unions, the CCF under David Lewis's direction, was able to convince many of the new CIO unions to hire CCF trade unionists as organizers, as the Communists had been doing for some time. This brought trade union questions much closer to the CCF itself, but it also brought the CCF trade union leaders into direct confrontation with their Communist opposite numbers.

The CCF at this point decided to seek direct affiliation from unions, and endorsation from the two trade union congresses.[11] In 1942, the convention of the CCL adopted a resolution which said "... that this Convention expresses its appreciation of the work done on behalf of labour by the CCF members in parliament and that it recommends to its chartered and affiliated unions that they study the program of the CCF." [12] But in 1943, the CCL went further and declared that it recognized the CCF as the political arm of labour in Canada and called upon all its unions to affiliate to the CCF.[13]

At the same time, an alliance developed between the Communist trade union officials and the Liberals. The Communist Party was illegal from June 6, 1940 until the end of the war, even though the Soviet Union had become an ally in the war against Germany and Italy after Hitler invaded Russia, June 22, 1941. Many of the leading Canadian Communists had been interned from the summer of 1940 until late in 1942, and were compelled to sign an affidavit pledging not to rejoin the party as a condition for their release. There was no other restriction and many resumed the active roles they had in the trade unions. In 1943, the Communists made a proposal directly to Mackenzie King, namely that the party be allowed to surface under a new name and in return it would co-operate in the trade unions with Liberals to impede the growth of affiliations of unions to the CCF. A memorandum to Mackenzie King from a member of his staff, dated July 15, 1943, stated:

> Whether the Government likes it or not, the industrial working class is being organized as never before, principally by the adherents of the CCF and Communists. Surely, it is good sense for the Government to bid for the solid backing of one of these elements.[14]

It was a short time afterwards that the *illegal* Communist Party emerged as the *legal* Labor-Progressive Party, and formed Liberal-Labor alliances in selected constituencies to run candidates, and as well, formed political action committees in Labour Councils, or at provincial and federal trade union conventions. But when the Ontario provincial elections took place on August 4, 1943, the labour vote went overwhelmingly for the candidates of the CCF:

	Vote	% of Vote	Seats
Progressive Conservative	469,672	35.7	38
C.C.F.	415,441	31.6	34
Liberal	406,064	30.9	16
Labor-Progressive (Communist)	31,812	2.4	2
		Total Seats	90

Gerald Caplan, in his history of the Ontario CCF, made this analysis:

> The majority of CCF votes were garnered in predominantly industrial constituencies, as were all its seats ... The CCF polled only 17% or about 82,000 of the rural votes ... It took 34 of the 50 urban seats, with an amazing 40% of the votes; the Conservatives polled 32%, the Liberals 26%. No fewer than 19 of the CCF's winning candidates were trade union members, ten belonging to TLC affiliates, nine to the CCL, two of whom were heads of their unions... The CCF's Toronto total was hurt by devastating defeats in Bellwoods and St. Andrew's; these two heavily ethnic working class ridings were won by Communists.[15]

The CCF was at last becoming a political force in Ontario. In fact, the 1943 results showed that the CCF in Ontario was ahead of its counterparts in the western provinces. It could justifiably boast that its efforts in the trade union movement since 1937 had produced this result. The working class of Ontario repudiated Hepburn's betrayal and Mackenzie King's wartime labour policies.

It was on February 17, 1944, a matter of no more than six months after the CCF victory in Ontario, that King enacted by Order-in-Council P.C. 1003, a national labour code, similar to the famous 1935 Wagner Act of Roosevelt's New Deal, which Canadian trade unions had been pressuring the King government to duplicate from the time that U.S. law was enacted.

The nature of the CCF victory was not a complete surprise, since a Gallup Poll released on March 27, 1943 predicted that if a provincial election were held in Ontario at that time, 26 percent of the electorate would vote CCF, as against a Conservative vote of 36 percent and a Liberal vote of 35 percent. Moreover, the same poll showed that the CCF could win in forty ridings.[16] The poll, the report said, also "makes it clear that the CCF is weakest on the farm."

The day after the election, E. B. Jolliffe, the Ontario leader of the CCF, rejected any suggestion that his party would try to assume governmental power with a minority of the seats in the Legislature. He was adamant in this position:

> I don't think that we should attempt to take office and carry out our program unless we have a clear working majority.
> — Interview in the *Toronto Star*, August 5, 1943.

The *Toronto Star*, in an editorial commenting on Jolliffe's interview, wrote that "his declaration clearly means that any party seeking a coalition with the CCF for a balance of power in the province must embrace the full CCF program and become in action, if not in name, members of the party."

A year later, Jolliffe made a radio broadcast in which he appeared to reverse his position:

> The CCF as the second largest group, is prepared to form a new government in Ontario if called upon to do so. (September 13, 1944)

In the aftermath of this apparent change, a resolution surfaced at a number of labour councils, followed by a full-page ad in the *Windsor Star* of September 25 calling for "a democratic coalition of the CCF, Liberal and Labor-Progressive Parties to defeat Drew."

This appeal was immediately denounced by Jolliffe as an emanation of the LPP, which it probably was, and he declared:

> The Tories would like to be the spearhead of reaction in this country but they are too weak to qualify. The real spearhead of reaction is the Liberal Party and it will get

the backing of the big interests because they know that the
Liberal Party alone has a national organization with some
chance of success.[17]

There could have been another option for the CCF, namely to
explore the possibility of the CCF as the government, legislating with
support from the Liberals on specific measures. It appeared that the
Ontario Liberal caucus would have agreed to such an arrangement.
Had the CCF pursued that path, it would have changed the face of
politics in Ontario, if not in the whole of Canada. As it was, the Drew
government, by copying many of the ideas in the famous Beveridge
Report, which had been published in Britain in December 1942,
opened the way for forty-two years of Tory rule in Ontario.

After the election in Ontario, the CCF was riding high in many
provinces, and on June 15, 1944 elected a government in the province
of Saskatchewan under the charismatic leader T. C. Douglas. That
government held power for twenty years, enacting some of the most
far-reaching social legislation ever to be implemented in a provincial
legislature.

These two elections showed that within ten years of its founding,
the CCF was becoming a major party in the Canadian political system. With respect to Saskatchewan, this could have been predicted in
view of the rise of the farmers' movements in that province, followed
by the Farmer-Labour Party, and the identification of three of the
most prominent CCFers, namely, Tommy Douglas, M. J. Coldwell,
and George H. Williams. But who could have forecast the stunning
victory in Ontario, where the CCF had few roots or leaders who were
well-known or charismatic?

But the victory in Ontario was short-lived. In the provincial election of June 4, 1945, the Conservatives under George Drew increased
from thirty-eight to sixty-six seats and their popular vote from 36
percent to 44 percent. A week later, in the federal general election,
the one federal seat which the CCF had won in Ontario in a by-election, February 9, 1942, was lost. On the other hand, in the West, the
CCF increased its seats in British Columbia from one to four, in
Saskatchewan from five to eighteen, and in Manitoba from one to
five, and retained its seat in Cape Breton in Nova Scotia. The Saskatchewan CCF, which became the government a year before, had
started to enact the program that it had promised, and evidently that
performance had pleased the voters there. The Ontario CCF, by re-
fusing to become the government, lost the chance of showing what it

could do. As a result, by June 1945, the CCF had returned to its status as a western party. Its percentage of the popular vote doubled from 8 percent in 1940 to 16 percent in 1945, due mainly to its increases in British Columbia where it received 30 percent; in Manitoba 32 percent, and in Saskatchewan 45 percent.

In September 1943, a month after the Ontario elections, the Gallup Poll predicted that if a general election were held at that time, the CCF nationally would get 29 percent of the vote as against the Liberals with 28 percent and the Progressive Conservatives also with 28 percent. This was the first and only time that the CCF had ever led the polls. What was the reason, then, for the sharp drop in support for the CCF within less than two years of this poll?

The Liberal and Conservative parties took the September 1943 polls as a warning to climb on the bandwagon of post-war reforms, as the CCF had done, particularly advocating the welfare state, which had become the main appeal for the people of Canada.

Drew made the welfare state the cornerstone of his July, 1943 "Twenty-Two Point Programme," which promised to look after the people's needs "from the cradle to the grave," and he pledged to implement this "in effective cooperation with the Dominion Government ..."

Mackenzie King established a Committee on Reconstruction, which was planning a Canadian version of Britain's Beveridge Report, and which had as its research director, Leonard Marsh, a member of the League for Social Reconstruction. It was also clear that such a plan of the federal government would require full co-operation from the provinces, as was done with the Unemployment Insurance Act for which King required the assent of all of them, or in shared-costs agreements. But family allowance, one of the points in the Marsh Report, was implemented by the federal government before the general elections. King decided to enact this as a straight federal "gift" to the mothers of Canada. This boosted the electoral prospects of the Liberal Party, because the first monthly cheques were to be delivered the beginning of July, three weeks after the election of June 11, 1945.

In a letter of November 4, 1943, David Lewis, national secretary of the CCF, stated that "it would be fairer to say that the two old Parties have given lip service to the idea of social security, but until recently neither of them made an issue of the subject or gave any concrete evidence of intention to implement it in practice. The CCF, on the other hand, has always placed social security in the forefront of its program, has spoken, written and propagandized on the subject, and has repeatedly declared its unshakable intention of introducing a program of social security at the first opportunity."[18]

But the indifference of the two old parties to social security disappeared in a few months after the September Gallup Poll, and the three parties were competing with each other from that point on. Mackenzie King produced his *Industry and Humanity* to prove that he had been for the welfare state as far back as 1918, when the book was published.[19]

The CCF had to face a barrage of propaganda unleashed primarily by Premier Drew, supplemented by what appeared to be an independent campaign, using advertisements in the daily press and the mails, spreading the most blatant slanders to convince the Ontario electorate that the CCF was a Communist party, planning to subvert and destroy the democratic way of life which Canadians had enjoyed up to that time. Anti-semitic attacks on David Lewis were included in this barrage. It was estimated at the time that the perpetrators of this campaign spent several million dollars, which was provided by many big corporations. The Communists levelled their own campaign against the CCF in 1944 in response to Jolliffe's refusal to join with them and with the Liberals to form a coalition government. In an editorial in the *Canadian Tribune* on December 16, 1944, the LPP declared:

> It seems clear that nothing less than repudiation of the CCF by the labour movement and a resounding defeat of the CCF at the polls, accompanied by the election of a powerful block of LPP, labor and independent MP's, together with any CCFers who take a pro-unity position, and reform Liberals, putting the Tories to decisive rout, can assure the achievement of a progressive Parliament and government in the next election.

The Labor-Progressive Party held its two seats in Toronto, but only one of its fifteen "Liberal-Labor" candidates was elected. They were defeated in three seats in the Windsor area, in which, as a result, the sitting CCF members were also defeated. In five other seats held by the CCF the presence of LPP candidates defeated the incumbents, including Jolliffe, the provincial leader.

From the day that the Soviet Union was attacked, the Canadian Communists advocated a national front behind Mackenzie King, submerging the class struggle, and the fight for socialism. The CCF, however, took the opposite position. Under the ideological leadership of M. J. Coldwell, president of the party, Frank Scott, professor of Law at McGill University, and David Lewis, national secretary, they published articles, pamphlets, and books setting out the socialist objectives of the CCF, with a new feeling of optimism about the postwar world. Much of this enthusiasm came from the British Labour Party, which believed that it would inherit the reins of government after the war; and by the example of the Soviet Union, which for the first time, the CCF leadership acknowledged, was a socialist society, and attributed its success on the battlefield to this fact.

The most important of the publications during this period were *Make This Your Canada*, written by David Lewis and Frank Scott (1943); *Planning for Freedom*, a book of essays, edited by the same two authors, who also contributed the first and last articles(1944); and *Left Turn, Canada* by M. J. Coldwell, published in England in 1945. In *Make This Your Canada*, Lewis and Scott wrote:

> Our own experience in the field of war production has been confirmed and emphasized by the accomplishments of the Soviet Union. The whole democratic world has been filled with admiration of the victorious struggles of the Red Army ... For some fifteen years before she was attacked, the Soviet Union had organized her economy in line with successive national plans based on the interests of all her people and the external dangers facing the country. Profit as the motive of production had long been eliminated. The techniques of the planned economy had been largely mastered not only by the experts but by the people themselves ...[20]

In explaining the nature of the socialist revolution in Russia because of the czarist oppression, the authors declared that "... this war has demonstrated beyond question that Soviet economic planning has built a powerful economy in a short space of time, and has won the enthusiastic support of the millions of people who inhabit that vast land." [21]

Because of the democratic traditions and the political party system in Canada, the path to socialism would be different, starting with the election of a CCF federal government, which would undertake at once the first stages of the transition from capitalism to socialism.

The first stage would emphasize the social legislation, such as pensions, family allowances, unemployment insurance, and guaranteed incomes "to bring tangible improvements to the great masses of the Canadian people. As this is done, the CCF will deserve and will gain an increasing support in the country which will ensure its return at the succeeding election." [22]

Taking over of the war economy, and the socialization of banks, railways, air and other major transportation facilities, public utilities, and basic manufacturing, would proceed quickly, and this would be the foundation for the socialist economy. Private enterprises of a smaller nature would continue to exist, as would co-operatives, and individual family-owned farms, but

> ... it should, however, be emphasized that the whole economy will come under the national plan and that every sector of it will have to play its part in the plan. Even enterprises which may be left in private hands will therefore function in accordance with the controls, regulations, and standards which the achievement of the plan will require. [23]

In an article in *Planning For Freedom,* written February 7, 1944, E. B. Jolliffe, leader of the Opposition in the Ontario Legislature, wrote "now that the CCF is approaching power, it has become more than ever necessary to be clear about our objectives." [24]

In his book, *Left Turn, Canada,* M. J. Coldwell, was still buoyed up by the prospects of a CCF government, even though the election of June 11, 1945 did not produce a CCF majority or anything close to it:

> We could not win this war if we relied on the individual whim of every industrialist, nor can we leave the post-war period to the tender mercies of the rugged individualist. This is the principle underlying the CCF viewpoint regarding post-war planning. It is the dividing line between the CCF and the other political parties, for Mr. Bracken, leader of the Progressive-Conservatives, Mr. Manning, the Social Credit Premier of Alberta, Mr. Tim Buck, leader of the Labor-Progressive (Communist) Party, and the spokesmen for the Mackenzie King Government, have all professed their allegiance to private enterprise as the basic principle of post-war reconstruction. [25]

But the predictions on which the CCF leadership was basing itself proved to be unfounded. There was no analysis of the political climate facing the CCF throughout the country. Even if the leaders had calculated on returns such as were won in the 1943 provincial elections in Ontario, there was nothing to suggest that a similar or even a somewhat smaller return from Quebec and the Maritime provinces could suddenly appear and produce seats for the CCF in those areas — nothing, that is, except their own enthusiasm. They calculated that the growing popularity of the British Labour Party and the certitude of its becoming the government after the war, would have a positive impact on the CCF. It did, but the circumstances were different. The Labour Party had emerged from the 1914–18 war as the second party, replacing the Liberals; it served as the government for two short periods, as well as in the wartime coalition under Winston Churchill from 1940. The impact of the Labour Party victory would have been greater on the CCF had the Canadian elections taken place after the British, rather than before. The growing admiration for the Soviet Union, based on the tremendous battles which the Red Army was winning, caused many to attribute these successes to the socialist system; as already noted, the CCF leaders joined in making this kind of evaluation. This might have had a more lasting impact on the CCF but for the outbreak of the cold war soon after, and the reversal of its own attitude to the Soviet system.

Mackenzie King won the election of June 11, 1945 by a small majority of two seats. He ascribed these results in part to his decision to implement some of the reform proposals which he had long talked about, in fact, had written about in *Industry and Humanity*. But the immediate decision to send out the first family allowance cheques was probably the factor that saved his small majority. He finally embarked on the road to reform because of the clear signal that the CCF had at last emerged as the chief advocate in the fight for the welfare state.

In the election campaign, that fight became the major issue not only between the Liberals and the CCF; even the Conservatives joined in on the action. But there was no doubt that the main beneficiary of this popular issue was Mackenzie King, as David Lewis pointed out in his memoirs:

> As the years roll by, there is a growing tendency for Liberals to take exclusive credit for the measures which the King government promised in 1945, some of which,

but not all, it implemented. I feel strongly about this because it is, from my personal and close observation, a
distortion of history not to recognize that it was the growing strength of the CCF which forced not only the Liberal
Party but the entire capitalist establishment to accept the
need for welfare legislation.[26]

The CCF increased its vote from the 1940 election total of 393,230
to the 1945 total of 816,260 or, in percentage figures, from 8.6 percent
to 15.6 percent. But an additional factor has to be considered, namely,
that in 1940 the CCF fielded only 96 candidates, while in 1945 it had
205. It increased its vote in Ontario from 61,000 to 261,000, but did
not elect a single candidate there, and only one from the Manitoba
border to Cape Breton. Its lowest vote by percentage was in Quebec,
where it had 2.4 percent. Its obvious source of satisfaction was Manitoba,
Saskatchewan, and British Columbia, but especially Saskatchewan
where it won 18 seats out of 21. That figure undoubtedly was due to
the support the CCF government was receiving from the voters of
that province since it took office in June 1944.

But an analysis of the campaign of the CCF in the 1945 federal
election showed that the CCF did not run on a reform platform, as
did the Liberals and to some extent the Conservatives. It ran on a
socialist platform, in which the reform measures were posited as part
of a socialist society, since only that could guarantee the success of
these reform measures. Placed in that context, people had to choose
between socialism and reformism. Moreover, by placing the achievements of the Soviet Union as an example of the planned socialist
economy, the CCF campaign must have alienated many people who
were not enamoured with the Soviet Union and with Josef Stalin.

Nevertheless, the election of 1945 firmly established the CCF as a
part of the Canadian political system, and that part of it that represented
the social-democratic ideology. Twelve years after the CCF was
founded, its doctrine as contained in the Regina Manifesto remained
intact, except for a temporary change in its attitude to the war. The CCF
leadership, which took over after the death of J. S. Woodsworth, not only
adhered to every word in the Manifesto, especially the phrase "the
eradication of capitalism," but in its conduct of the 1945 campaign,
it strengthened its public image as the party of socialism.

6

The Transition from CCF to NDP

The period from 1945 to 1961 was particularly difficult for the CCF national leadership. Confronted with the cold war, in which the former allies of the Soviet Union had become its enemies, the CCF was compelled to reverse its praise of the socialism of the Soviet Union. Frank Scott, national chairman, in opening the CCF's Eleventh National Convention in July 1950, expressed this revised evaluation accordingly:

> The Communist Party [of the Soviet Union — NP] has no right to the word socialist, since what it calls "scientific socialism" is the negation of the most fundamental part of socialism, namely its respect for the individual human being...We now see that it is possible for a country to nationalize all the means of production and still be as far from socialism as ever.[1]

He did not suggest that the Regina Manifesto be replaced or changed at this Convention, but he did propose some formulations that would need to be overhauled in the future:

> ...I suggest that for any socialist today to look upon every proposal for nationalization as the acid test of true socialism, an act of faith rather than of reason, is to be a little foolish...While our fundamental purpose of production for use remains, we must keep an open and intelligent

mind on the problem of the degree and timing of socialization.[2]

He also proposed a relaxation of the hitherto firm CCF position on
centralization:

> Let those who accuse us of an undue desire for centrali-
> zation take note: we must strike a balance, separating out
> the functions appropriate to federal action, from those
> appropriate to provinces and municipalities...the CCF
> must support a flexible method for amending the B.N.A.
> Act, except for matters which may be considered fun-
> damental human and minority rights.[3]

He attributed this proposal to the record of the CCF government
in Saskatchewan, which had already demonstrated the importance of
a province in carrying out a socialist program, "though it has also
shown the limitations."

But the significant changes in the Manifesto did not occur until the
Winnipeg Convention in 1956. The Regina Manifesto became the
"Winnipeg Declaration of Principles of the Co-operative Commonwealth Federation," and the difference was illustrated in the final
paragraphs:

> *1933*:
> No CCF Government will rest content until it has eradi-
> cated capitalism and put into operation the full programme
> of socialized planning which will lead to the establishment
> in Canada of the Co-operative Commonwealth.

> *1956*:
> The CCF will not rest content until every person in this
> and in all other lands is able to enjoy equality and freedom,
> a sense of human dignity, and an opportunity to live a rich
> and meaningful life as a citizen of a free and peaceful
> world.

There was an important change in language between the two, but
it was more than that. Basically, it was a change in orientation, from
a doctrinaire to a less rigid approach.

The 1933 text stated that the only way to achieve the goals of the CCF was through the "eradication of capitalism," whereas the 1956 document omitted any statement of means, and settled for a restatement of aims such as "equality," "freedom," "human dignity," and "a rich and meaningful life."

There was a heated debate, as expected, but in the end the Winnipeg Declaration of Principles passed, relegating the Regina Manifesto to the archives, along with the CCF literature of the war, especially *Make This* Your *Canada*, *Planning for Freedom*, and *Left Turn, Canada*.

This was not a sudden shift, but rather the cumulative result of ten years of rethinking, brought on by a steady decline in the CCF's percentage of votes, even though the total vote for CCF candidates was increasing. In 1949, the percentage of the popular vote for the CCF fell from 15.6 to 13.4; in 1953 it was 11.3; in 1957 it dropped to 10.7; and 1958 it was reduced to 9.5, almost to the level the CCF obtained in its first election in 1935.

Although the CCF supported the external and military policies of the cold war, it became a victim as well. Socialism had become unpopular, especially as a result of the propaganda emanating from Washington, and more particularly from the American trade union leadership, both in the AFL and the CIO. The CCF co-operated with the main trade union officers in the USA as well as in Canada in removing Communists from the leadership of several important unions, and where this was impossible, expelling entire unions from the CCL or TLC.[4] This made it easier for a transformed CCF to win endorsation of a merged trade union centre, as well as the affiliation of a number of powerful industrial unions.

But on the way to this desired goal the CCF changed its outlook and its statement of principles. It would have been impossible for the Canadian Labour Congress, founded in 1956 as a result of the merger of the two major trade union centres, to endorse the CCF or its successor on the basis of the Regina Manifesto. The major reason for this was the number of trade unions, particularly of the AFL, which might be able to ignore the old Gompers's ban on unions joining political parties, but never with such an explicit socialist orientation. The two centres had at that time well over a million members between them, a majority of whom voted in federal elections for candidates of the Liberal Party. It would have been much more difficult to persuade them not to oppose the CCF, or its successor, with the Regina Manifesto.

At the CCF convention of 1956, the guest speaker was Richard Crossman, of the British Labour Party, whose speech was approved warmly by David Lewis at the time and in his memoirs:

> Ironically enough, it is the socialists and the trade unions of the world who have saved capitalism, from its inevitable collapse by raising the standard of living of the masses of the people and so providing the purchasing power which was required to create a new form of capitalism, such as we see it today.[5]

This speech was part of an ideological assault on the tenets of social-democratic thought as they had been understood through the depression and in the immediate post-war years by the socialist parties of Western Europe and Britain. Crossman, referred to by Lewis as "one of the moderate leftists of the British Labour Party"; John Strachey, a former Marxist, and as with Crossman, a cabinet minister in the Attlee Government, author of the 1956 book *Contemporary Capitalism*; and Harold Laski, long-time leading figure in the intellectual left, were among the more prominent spokesmen who were "re-thinking socialism" at this time. David Lewis, in his advocacy of this approach, added a "new principle" out of the Canadian experience:

> I have often said that to a CCF'er, the winning of an election is of course tremendously important. The achievement of power in a province and in the country is what we are giving all our efforts and all our energies to. But even more important than becoming the government, even more important than the achievement of power, is the achievement of decent legislation for the Canadian people day by day, and week by week on the road to power, and that achievement the CCF has to its credit in this country.[6]

Another factor in explaining this revamping, was the Stalin revelations in the report by Nikita Khrushchev at the Twentieth Congress of the Communist Party of the Soviet Union (CPSU) in February 1956, and which was referred to by Crossman, Strachey, and Laski.[7] It was no longer possible, if it ever had been, to call the Soviet Union a socialist, let alone a Marxist, state. But could this justify arguments which suggested that the purpose of social democracy is to improve the capitalist society, or that a CCF party is not mainly interested in becoming the government but rather in convincing the existing capitalist parties to legislate on behalf of the ordinary people?

The two figures who influenced British social democracy during and after the Second World War were not social democrats, but reform-minded economists, Sir William Beveridge and Sir J. M. Keynes. The former fashioned the most complete model of a welfare state. Keynes projected the role of the state in a capitalist economy, whereby it pours money into job creation during a downturn, and relies on the capitalists to invest in capital and consumer goods in times of upswing. They also influenced the leaders of the CCF, and by the time of its 1956 convention the party seemed ready to abandon what it considered "doctrinaire socialism," to a more acceptable social democracy, by which Lewis meant "a mixed economy." He made it clear that the CCF had to recognize that "public ownership is a means to be used wherever the circumstances make it necessary and only to the extent that it is necessary...Public ownership in a democratic society and under a democratic socialist government will never cover more than a part of the economy..."[8]

David Lewis and many of the CCF trade union leaders saw the eventual formation of the Canadian Labour Congress as an historic opportunity to ally the new trade union centre with the CCF, and they began to work in that direction. The election of Claude Jodoin, an officer of the International Ladies' Garment Workers (AFL) in Quebec, as the first president of the CLC, provided considerable impetus to this goal. He was very friendly to the CCF, and supported a connection between the CCF and CLC.

But inside the CCF there was strong opposition. Stanley Knowles, MP, in a letter to Harold Winch, British Columbia provincial leader of the CCF, dated August 18, 1957, argued against affiliation:

> I'd say the arguments for a new vehicle are less strong now than they were when the CLC was formed. It takes a long time to get a party to the place where it gets 10-11% of the popular vote. The spread between our 11% and the PC's 39% is not an impossible gulf. But for a new vehicle to start at zero and get nowhere is a different story.[9]

A little more than a year later, he reversed this opinion. A National Committee for A New Party (NCNP) was established, with ten rep-

resentatives from the CCF and ten from the CLC, with Stanley
Knowles, now a vice-president of the CLC, as chairman. Probably
the main factor in causing Knowles to change was the decline in CCF
votes and seats in the 1958 elections, including his own defeat in
Winnipeg North Centre. The CCF vote in that election was 9.5 percent of the popular vote and eight seats, a heavy setback as compared
with the 1957 results of 10.7 percent and twenty-five seats. In 1957
the distribution of CCFers elected to the House of Commons was
three in Ontario, five in Manitoba, ten in Saskatchewan, and seven in
British Columbia. In 1958, in the election on March 31, less than nine
months after, the CCF's distribution was three in Ontario, none in
Manitoba, one in Saskatchewan, and four in British Columbia. Many
CCFers, including some of the leaders, felt that the party was back
where it started in 1935, when it received 8.7 percent of the vote, and
seven seats.

But this was not the case, even though the setback was real. In
1935, in its first campaign, the CCF received 385,000 votes; in 1958,
700,000 votes. In Saskatchewan, the CCF was entrenched as the
government; in British Columbia, it was the official opposition; in the
Manitoba Legislature it held eleven seats. Nevertheless, the federal
election of 1958 was the deciding factor in the movement towards a
new party. In the Second Convention of the Canadian Labour Congress, April 1958, a resolution was passed by an overwhelming vote
authorizing the executive to begin negotiations to establish a new
political party:

> The time has come for a fundamental re-alignment of
> political forces in Canada. There is need for a broadly
> based people's political movement, which embraces the
> CCF, the labour movement, farm organizations, pro-
> fessional people and other liberally minded persons inter-
> ested in basic social reform and reconstruction through our
> parliamentary system of government...[10]

It appeared that the initiative came from the labour movement to
establish a new party, but that was not the case. David Lewis was the
prime mover in bringing the CCF and the CLC together, and he had
arranged most of the steps that were taken on the way. When the party
was assembled for the launching in 1961, he appreciated better than
most the background of that historic moment; he also knew the
difficulties that lay ahead.

The resolution of the CLC projected a political party that was unreal. By the time of the founding convention, the farm organizations had decided not to join any political party. The reference to "professional people and other liberally minded persons" was ambiguous. None of the organizations of professional people joined, nor were they approached to join. The CCF responded of course as did the main section of the labour movement. The Quebec-based successor to the Catholic unions, the Confederation of National Trade Unions (the Confédération des syndicats nationaux), refused to join, mainly due to its rivalry with the Canadian Labour Congress. The CCF and the CLC were there, and that was enough to launch the NDP.

What was surprising, however, was the lack of any real opposition from what used to be the Trades and Labour Congress, and from the international offices of the AFL. The resolution might have been just a gesture, but the election of Knowles to be a vice-president of the CLC with its responsibility for negotiating the new party, indicated that the CLC intended to help bring about the new party with all possible speed.

The formal unity between the CLC and the CCF in a new party was accomplished within three years. The founding convention of the New Democratic Party took place between July 31 and August 4, 1961 with close to 2,000 delegates, and amidst great enthusiasm.

The program that was adopted differed from the Regina Manifesto and the Winnipeg Declaration. It was more of an election platform than a manifesto, which stressed immediate reforms rather than long-term objectives. It had no reference to socialism or social democracy; it balanced the jurisdictions between the federal and provincial governments, and therefore appeared to be less centralist than the CCF. The status of French Canada was presented in a new light:

> ... Our pride in Canada as a nation is enhanced by our consciousness of the two national cultures which form the basis of Canadian life. We are indeed aware that those who have their roots in the French-speaking community frequently and legitimately use the word "nation" to describe French Canada itself. The New Democratic Party believes that true Canadian unity depends upon equal recognition and respect for both the main cultures of our country.

The change in orientation, which began in the 1956 Declaration of Principles of the CCF, was continued and extended in the program adopted by the New Democratic Party, as a compromise necessary to bring about a merger of labour and the CCF. In a way this was a repetition of the formation of the British Labour Party in 1906, when the socialist organizations, in their effort to unite with the Trades Union Congress in a political instrument independent of the Liberal and Conservative parties, had to eliminate all references to socialism in order to gain the approval of the leaders of the British trade union movement.

It would appear that the CLC resolution of 1958 calling for a new party to attract diverse sections of the Canadian people, including "liberally minded people," had in mind many of the leaders of the CLC, especially of the AFL. Stanley Knowles was surprised to learn that Frank Hall, a leader of the Canadian section of the AFL Brotherhood of Railway and Steamship Clerks, and a long-time enemy of the CCF, "became very enthusiastic" about the new party.[11]

The top officers of the Canadian Congress of Labour and their CIO affiliates had endorsed the CCF in 1943 and were ready and anxious to transfer their political aims to the new party.

The compromises that had to be made to bring about the new party were mainly the result of pressure from the former leaders of the Trades and Labour Congress and the AFL in Canada. The fact, however, that they finally agreed to endorse the new party was a step forward in labour's role in Canadian politics.

The leading personnel of the new party and the dominant movers at the convention were the former leaders of the CCF, without exception: Tommy Douglas, Hazen Argue, David Lewis, Frank Scott, Harold Winch, Woodrow Lloyd, Donald MacDonald, Charles Millard, and Stanley Knowles, among others. There were no leading people representing the farm movements, the professional organizations, "and other liberally minded persons." But the absence from the leadership of trade unionists who had never endorsed the CCF, yet openly supported the NDP, such as Claude Jodoin, was conspicuous, even though Jodoin had made it clear that neither he nor other prominent labour leaders would occupy leading positions in the new party.[12]

This absence continued to be a characteristic of the NDP, with some exceptions, mainly from the auto workers union, whose leading figures such as Dennis McDermott (later president of the CLC) and Robert White, played an important public role in the party. Nevertheless, the impact of the changed relationship between the CCF and the CLC as brought about by the creation of the New Democratic Party was, from the outset, of major importance. It settled the question of which party would be the legislative and political arm of the labour movement, thus ending the fratricidal conflict that had been waged between the CCF, the Communists, and the Liberals over that question. It made available financial assistance of a substantial kind for the NDP, from the treasuries of many big unions and from the dues of affiliated unions.

But the crucial question of how many additional votes could be attributed to the merger, could not be gauged accurately. In the federal elections from 1962 on, the NDP elected between five and eleven members from Ontario, with approximately 20 percent of the votes; British Columbia, usually more than ten seats and over 30 percent of the votes; Manitoba averaged five seats and 27 percent of the votes. However, Saskatchewan was a disappointment until 1968, failing to elect any candidates in 1962, 1963, and 1965. In provincial elections, the NDP was able to elect governments in British Columbia in 1972, 1991; in Manitoba in 1969, 1973, 1981, 1986; in Saskatchewan 1971, 1975, 1978, 1991; and Ontario in 1990. But in all the other provinces, both in federal and in provincial elections, the NDP could not break through, with minor exceptions, such as winning one seat in a 1979 federal by-election in Newfoundland, one seat held twice in Nova Scotia's Cape Breton, and one in the Northwest Territories, where the NDP has elected one person to the House of Commons in each election since 1972, with the exception of 1980, and one by-election in a Quebec riding in 1990. In other words, the changeover from CCF to NDP has been accompanied by electoral gains at the federal and provincial levels, but it is difficult to establish whether this was due to the ties with labour, or was a part of the slow process of the evolution of social democracy in Canada.

The last election for the CCF was in 1958 and was considered to be a disaster. The total vote for all its candidates was 692,398, which constituted 9.5 percent of the popular vote.

The 1962 election, the first under the banner of the New Democratic Party, resulted in 1,036,853 votes for the NDP, or 13.5 percent of the total votes cast, and the election of nineteen members. This was the largest vote for social democracy in Canada, although not in terms of percentages; the 1945 federal election had resulted in 15.6 percent of the popular vote and twenty-eight seats for the CCF.

Yet in some important aspects the composition of the vote was different. In 1945, the CCF carried eighteen of twenty-one seats in Saskatchewan; in 1962, the NDP, with T. C. Douglas as its national leader, did not win a single seat in that province, nor in the next two elections. On the other hand, the NDP won six seats in Ontario, of which three were in Northern Ontario and three in Metropolitan Toronto, and slowly increased this number over the years. In British Columbia, the NDP also continued a slow growth in the federal elections, ranging from ten seats in 1962 to nineteen in 1988. Manitoba had similar results, although these oscillated more than other strongholds of the CCF-NDP.

The NDP, in this respect, inherited a pattern that started even before the CCF, when certain ridings became "safe seats" for their social-democratic incumbents. The two labour members of the House of Commons elected in 1921, J. S. Woodsworth from Winnipeg Centre (later North Centre) and William Irvine in Calgary East, were joined by A. A. Heaps in 1925 in Winnipeg North and in 1930 by Angus MacInnis from Vancouver East. Winnipeg North Centre has been Labour, CCF, and NDP up until 1984, with one exception. The standard-bearers there were J. S. Woodsworth and Stanley Knowles. Winnipeg North was carried by A. A. Heaps, Alistair Stewart, and David Orlikow from 1945 until 1988. Vancouver East has been held by Angus MacInnis, Harold Winch and Margaret Mitchell from 1930 to the present (1988). Regier, Douglas, and Svend Robinson from 1957 have done the same in Burnaby-Coquitlam. Andrew Brewin, Bob Rae, and Lynn McDonald were elected in the Toronto-Greenwood riding from 1962 until Lynn McDonald's defeat in 1988. Herridge, Harding, Kristiansen were elected in Kootenay West from 1945 on, with one exception. Frank Howard and Jim Fulton in the Skeena constituency from 1957 until the present; Ed Broadbent, after being elected for the first time in Oshawa in 1968, was returned at every election, and when he resigned in 1990 was replaced by a colleague, Micheal Breaugh.

From 1962, when the NDP first contested the federal elections, its total vote across the country was never less than a million, whereas under the CCF, it never reached that figure.

NDP VOTES IN FEDERAL ELECTIONS

1962	1,036,853	13.5%	1974	1,476,360	15.0%
1963	1,037,857	13.1%	1979	2,024,452	18.0%
1965	1,381,658	17.9%	1980	2,203,103	20.0%
1968	1,378,389	17.0%	1984	2,401,280	19.0%
1972	1,393,292	16.4%	1988	2,633,665	20.0%[13]

The ability of the NDP to increase its popular vote up to 2.6 million in the latest federal election, is due to a number of factors, not the least of which is the expanding treasury that permitted the party to field candidates in practically every riding in the country. Undoubtedly, this is one of the benefits of the close connection with the CLC and its affiliates.

The election of 1988 showed that the electorate was still divided in its perceptions of the NDP. In the Atlantic provinces the vote for NDP candidates was always low. In Quebec, the vote showed a substantial increase though not enough to elect a candidate. Ontario, Manitoba, Saskatchewan, and British Columbia elected a considerable number of MPs, plus one from the Yukon, and one from Alberta for a total of forty-three, the largest number of NDP members ever.

In the past four general elections, the votes in Quebec for the NDP candidates show the following:

1979	163,492	5.1%	1984	301,928	8.8%
1980	268,409	9.1%	1988	487,971	14.0%

The voting support of the NDP in Quebec tripled in less than ten years, and in a by-election on February 12, 1990, it gained its first seat from a francophone riding there, with a vote of 66 percent of the total poll.

The close connection between the NDP and the CLC was not reflected in the class composition of the MPs as shown in the parliamentary caucus in 1988, including the addition of the by-election in Quebec in 1990:

> 3 farmers; 6 lawyers; 5 workers; 7 teachers; 6 social workers; 13 professionals (consultants, accountants, civil service, etc.); 2 Protestant ministers; 2 professors (1 Arts, 1 Science) — TOTAL 44[14]

As in the British Labour Party, there appears to be a division of functions between the parliamentary wing and the trade unions, at least with respect to full-time union officials. There are no prominent trade union leaders in the caucus, nor have they been candidates. This was not so conspicuous when David Lewis was alive, because of his very close connections with the top leaders of the trade unions in Canada and the United States. But this closeness had negative as well as positive aspects, especially during the so-called Waffle period. But from the point of view of economic policy, this is the one area which the trade union leaders guard jealously. When Ed Broadbent deviated from trade union orthodoxy, the CLC forced a retraction. The immediate issue was a formula by James Laxer, which Broadbent endorsed, that the emphasis should be to replace the demand for consumer goods and services with a new policy based on the needs of production, even at the expense of the consumers.[15]

In the period from its founding in 1961 to 1968 the NDP added two policies to the customary programs and platforms of the CCF. One was the recognition of the national status of French Canada, the other an increasing emphasis on Canadian economic independence from the United States.

In a Federal Council meeting, November 20, 1964, the NDP adopted a Statement on Confederation which altered its position on Quebec, beginning with the declaration that

> Canada today faces a crisis which may well result in the break-up of Confederation and the disintegration of our nation.

It repeated its familiar declarations that "the federal government must have all the authority necessary to deal with matters of national concern ..." but inserted a section headed "The Special Case of Quebec":

> 10. We share the view of Quebec that the preservation and development of French culture and tradition require a strong provincial government and a special consideration in Confederation.

> 11. Quebec can, if she wishes to, elect to separate from Canada, but we believe that she will not do so. Separation would benefit neither Quebec nor the rest of Canada, and would place both economies at a serious disadvantage.

12. We feel it is not only possible but desirable to work out a status for Quebec within Confederation which recognizes her special tradition and culture. But this can only be based on a reciprocal recognition by Quebec that a strong and lasting Confederation requires certain basic matters of national concern to be left to the jurisdiction of the federal government.[16]

The NDP and the Quiet Revolution in Quebec arrived on the scene at approximately the same time in Canadian history, and social democracy was one of the strong currents in the upsurge in Quebec, where it had been suppressed by the ultramontane wing of the Catholic church, which had dominated the ideology of Quebec for over a hundred years.

The emphasis on economic independence from the United States was accentuated by two professors who became public figures in the mid-1960s. Kari Levitt, a professor of economics at McGill, was working on a series of papers on the growth of direct American investment in Canadian industry, both primary and secondary, when she was invited by David Lewis to present a paper on this subject to a Federal Council meeting in June 1966.[17] She made a deep impression at that time, and appeared again at a Federal Council in December 1968. Her findings were published in 1970 in the book *Silent Surrender*.[18] The well-known political scientist Leon Dion said this:

The devastating thesis of Kari Levitt concerning the American domination of Canada, notably through the complex role of the multinational corporations, has greatly reinforced the convictions of the spokesmen of socialist and social-democratic nationalism on this question ...[19]

In January 1968, Walter Gordon, a member of Pearson's government, released the Report of a Task Force on Canadian Industry, which he had established under the direction of Melville Watkins, professor of political economy at the University of Toronto and at that time a Liberal. The national leader of the NDP, T. C. Douglas, on behalf of the national executive, issued a press release dated February 16, 1968, welcoming the Task Force Report:

> The Watkins Report is a serious indictment of the economic policies pursued by Canadian governments and industry. The evidence and analysis contained in the Report fully justify the demands of the New Democratic Party for an energetic program designed to reduce foreign control of our economy and to require all industry, including foreign subsidiaries, to operate in the interests of Canada rather than those of another country.[20]

A few weeks later, at a Federal Council meeting in Winnipeg, the NDP reiterated its support for the Watkins Report:

> ...the Report had produced strong confirmation of the NDP belief that Canadians do not have control of their own economy and ... that no other western industrialized nation has so great a degree of foreign control of its industry.[21]

These statements persuaded a number of young intellectuals in or around the NDP to make the party more nationalistic, more socialist, and more anti-American. Mel Watkins joined the NDP and became one of the leaders in a new movement which was emerging within the NDP, and which in a few months became known as "The Waffle."

Many developments took place within a short space of time, including the resignation of T. C. Douglas, the close battle for the leadership between David Lewis and James Laxer, one of the leaders of the Waffle, the expulsion from the NDP of the Waffle, the retirement of Lewis and the rise of Ed Broadbent, who was elected leader of the party in 1975.

Even before the election of 1968 there was an undercurrent of dissatisfaction with Douglas's leadership, mainly from Ontario, and particularly from the trade union chiefs. The 1968 federal elections indicated that in Saskatchewan the NDP had regained its former power and strength after a virtual desert for the three previous elections. But Douglas himself was defeated in the Burnaby-Seymour riding in British Columbia.

In February 1968, Stephen Lewis went out to meet Tommy Douglas in British Columbia for the express purpose of asking him to step down from the leadership.[22] Douglas said he would consider it, but not if it would result in David Lewis's becoming the leader rather than a younger person.

Douglas finally rejected Stephen Lewis's request, declaring that he would stay on for one more convention, which would be held in 1969, and could assure his party that he would give up the leadership in 1971. In a letter to the party's federal secretary, dated May 6th, 1969, he made it clear that he would resign at the next convention even though "New Democratic Party organizations at the federal and constituency level have asked me to allow my name to go before our Biennial Convention next October."[23] There is no doubt that at the convention which replaced him, Douglas supported one or more of the younger candidates, although publicly he was pledged to neutrality. He had made it clear to people close to him that he hoped that some one would emerge other than David Lewis, not because of any dislike or disagreement with him, but because he believed it was time for a new type of leader. He was influenced in this by the election of the charismatic Pierre Trudeau as head of the Liberal Party in 1968, much younger than Douglas or Lewis, and perceived to have a fresh new outlook.

But between the dissatisfaction with Douglas as leader, which surfaced in 1968, and the convention in 1971 which replaced him, the Waffle appeared, and for a short period rocked the party as no previous schism had before in the history of social-democratic movements in Canada.

The Waffle emerged out of the world-wide youth revolt in the 1960s directed at the U.S. invasion of Vietnam, the Quiet Revolution in Quebec, and the growing awareness in Canada of the consequences of direct American investment in Canadian industry and resources. It announced its arrival with a Manifesto for an Independent Socialist Canada which declared:

> Our aim as democratic socialists is to build an independent socialist Canada. Our aim as supporters of the New Democratic Party is to make it a truly socialist party ... The major threat to Canadian survival today is American control of the Canadian economy. The major issue of our times is not national unity but national survival, and the fundamental threat is external, not internal ... But economic independence without socialism is a sham, and neither are meaningful without true participatory democracy.[24]

A glaring omission was the lack of Quebec francophones among the signatories to the Manifesto, except for one. Nevertheless, it did contain a statement of concern about Quebec to the effect that "there is no denying the existence of two nations within Canada, each with its own language, culture and aspirations. This reality must be incorporated into the strategy of the New Democratic Party ..."

Throughout the following two years the Waffle was very active, vocal, and visible. The activists wrote and published numerous declarations, held press conferences, organized their own meetings, and were able to win several NDP nominations in the elections as "NDP-Waffle" candidates. Before long, they appeared to many as the beginning of a new party.

This was becoming intolerable to some of the leaders of the NDP, but they did not try to restrict these activities until the Wafflers went a step too far by launching an all-out campaign against the trade union leaders, who were accused of being agents of American capitalism and toadies of the U.S. State Department.

By equating the trade unions that had their headquarters in the United States to all other "branch plants," they provoked the Canadian leaders of these unions to demand that the NDP take action against the Waffle.

A trade union columnist in the *Toronto Star*, who was very sympathetic to the Waffle, and an officer of a Canadian union in the CLC, wrote:

> The latest manifestation of the internationals' excessive influence within the NDP was the recent joint attack on the left-wing Waffle group by the federal and Ontario party leaders, David and Stephen Lewis. Their decision to start a purge of the Waffle was mainly a response to pressure from the Steelworkers, the United Auto Workers, and other American unions ... the internationals have, in effect, given the NDP an ultimatum: Either the Waffle goes, or we go.
>
> — Ed Finn, *The Toronto Star* 3 April 1972

In a short space of time the Waffle had sizeable support within and around the NDP. This was shown in the contest for leadership at the convention of April 24, 1971. At the outset, there were five candidates: David Lewis MP, James Laxer (a young history student at Queen's and leader of the Waffle), John Harney, Ed Broadbent MP, and Frank Howard MP. On the fourth and last ballot, David Lewis won with 1,046 against James Laxer's 612.

It was a victory for Lewis, but a very strong and surprising result for Laxer. There is no doubt that his votes were not all cast in support of the Waffle program. Some voted for Laxer as a younger man or out of opposition to Lewis. According to the *Toronto Star*, April 26, 1971, there were 490 delegates at the convention from trade unions, and the vast majority voted for Lewis, which meant that the votes of the delegates from riding associations were split 50-50 between Lewis and Laxer.

Shortly after, Stephen Lewis, at that time Ontario leader, and his father David Lewis, national leader, began their campaign to oust the Waffle or to emasculate its ability to function within the framework of the NDP. In June 1972, they issued an ultimatum containing no concessions to the Waffle as a group but permitting the members to remain within the NDP as long as they agreed to adhere to the rules. The majority of Wafflers decided to withdraw from the NDP and form the "Movement for an Independent Socialist Canada" (MISC) which petered out within two years. It became evident, once they left the NDP, that their main strength had come from their membership in the NDP, not outside of it.

Nevertheless, the policies which the Waffle stood for, have remained in no small measure in the NDP: opposition to free trade, advocacy of the national rights of Quebec, and the growing support for Canadianizing unions.

The New Democratic Party in Quebec

The change from CCF to NDP did not produce any notable growth in the party's fortunes in Quebec, at least until the federal elections of 1988, when it obtained close to 500,000 votes, or 14 percent of the total. It showed surprising results in many francophone ridings, and ran a close second in six: Abitibi, Chambly, Champlain, Lac-St-Jean, Saint-Maurice, and Temiscamingue. In the other sixty-nine ridings, the average vote for NDP candidates was 6,100, which was also a record. In a by-election in Chambly, on February 12, 1990, the NDP candidate, Phil Edmonston, who had placed second in 1988 with 17,268 votes, won the seat with 26,998 votes, a first for the NDP.

The Quiet Revolution in Quebec, which most historians date from the defeat of the Union nationale in June 22, 1960, had brought enormous changes in that province, but did not result in any significant way in support for the NDP. The first big change was the end of the repressive regime of Duplessis' party and with it the power of the more conservative bishops. But a number of events had preceded it, which clearly showed Quebec beginning to emerge from the control of reactionary forces: the radicalization of the Catholic syndicates, the Abestos strike of 1949, the public appearance of a group of young intellectuals, Catholics but independent of the political influence of the Church, such as Pierre Trudeau, Jean Marchand, René Lévesque, Gérard Pelletier, Paul Gerin-Lajoie, Pierre Laporte; and the appearance of several separatist movements.

The political developments accelerated, and the Quebec Liberal party under Jean Lesage entered the 1960 election as a coalition, which included radical nationalists such as René Lévesque, Paul Gerin-Lajoie, and Pierre Laporte, who demanded basic reforms and succeeded in winning many of them during the six years in office. The privately-owned electric power utilities were nationalized and Quebec Hydro created. A Ministry of Education was inaugurated, thus placing education under state control, rather than under the Church. Labour legislation was introduced to give unions the democratic rights they had been denied; the civil service and the teachers were granted union rights; social measures which had been so neglected under Duplessis were instituted, culminating in the historic Quebec Pension Plan, and many other reforms. It was, in fact, the heyday of democracy in Quebec.

VOTES FOR THE NDP IN QUEBEC FEDERAL ELECTIONS

YEAR	VOTES	%	YEAR	VOTES	%	YEAR	VOTES	%
1962	91,795	4.4	1963	151,061	7.5	1965	244,339	12.0
1968	164,466	7.5	1972	168,910	6.4	1974	162,080	6.6
1979	163,492	5.1	1980	268,409	9.1	1984	301,928	8.8
1988	487,971	14.0						

There were other important developments before the end of the decade: the formation of an underground Front de libération du Québec (FLQ) and the beginning of its terrorist activities; the election of Pierre Trudeau as leader of the federal Liberal Party and prime minister; the foundation of the Parti Quebecois, led by René Lévesque, with the goal of separating Quebec from the rest of Canada.

Socialism, social democracy, and Marxism, which had been looked upon as forbidden doctrines, now flourished in the French and English universities. Organizations, journals and periodicals which based themselves on these doctrines were launched and attracted thousands of francophones. The atmosphere was characterized by speed, turmoil, rising militancy, and Quebec-based nationalism, all of which left the old-style Quebec politics in a shambles.

This affected the CCF and its successors. In 1955, the party changed its name in Quebec to the "Parti social-democratique" (PSD) and in 1963 it changed again, this time to the "Parti Socialiste du Québec" (PSQ). But the change in name, which applied only to the provincial organization, did not improve the status of the party, nor did the recruitment into the leadership of some important Quebeckers, such as Robert Cliche, Raymond Laliberté, and Romeo Mathieu.

The main problem with the NDP, as with its predecessor, the CCF, was its inability to come to terms with the nationalism in Quebec, or with the continued domination there of its anglophone leaders, such as David Lewis, Frank Scott, and Charles Taylor. This was complicated by the deep-seated centralization embedded in its programs: the Regina Manifesto (1933), the Winnipeg Declaration of Principles (1956), and the New Party Declaration (1961). It did make some concessions to provincial rights in this latter document, but sentiment in Quebec had already moved beyond that. In fact, the pattern of social-democratic thought and action in Quebec kept advancing, while the NDP's position lagged behind.

This is not to suggest that the NDP could have endorsed the separatist position of René Lévesque because his domestic platform was social-democratic. But it could have revised its position on Quebec's rights. Pierre Trudeau, in a 1960 farewell to the CCF, made this comment about its rigidity on Canadian federalism:

> ... the CCF has reaped little electoral reward for its studied application in speaking with one voice and acting with one purpose in all parts of Canada. In Quebec alone, where the socialist vote has usually hovered around one per cent of the total, a book could be filled with the frustrations of former members of the CCF who felt or imagined that provincial affairs must always be subordinate to the *raison d'Etat* of the national party.[1]

Later, Trudeau as prime minister changed, and when he introduced the Charter of Rights on television, October 2, 1980, he made it clear that this major revision to the BNA Act would be submitted to the British parliament without seeking the approval of the Canadian provinces. It would be legal, according to him, for the Canadian Parliament by itself to amend and patriate the Constitution and for the British parliament to agree to this, without any debate:

> ...the Canadian people must now find a way of breaking out of fifty-three years of constitutional paralysis ... There is such a way. It is a legal way, though it demands collective determination: through the one institution in which all Canadians are represented, the Parliament of Canada. Canadians can break the deadlock among their eleven governments.[2]

But Trudeau eventually had to retreat on this as a result of the landmark decision of the Supreme Court of September 28, 1981, which ruled that amendments to the Constitution which involved the transfer of powers from provinces to the federal government, ought to have the assent of "a substantial number of the provinces." After a bitter struggle, the anglophone provinces finally agreed to sign the Charter of Rights, but not until Trudeau had yielded to their demand for the inclusion of a "notwithstanding" clause.[3]

But Broadbent and the Federal Council of the NDP consistently supported Trudeau's position, even after his secret meeting during the night of November 4, 1981 with the anglophone first ministers, from which the Quebec government had been excluded. In other words, the anglophone leadership of the NDP demonstrated its lack of solidarity with the Quebec left, which denounced Trudeau's package as a denial of Quebec's basic right of self-determination. Nevertheless, when the revised constitutional package was debated in the House, November 30, 1981, Broadbent proposed an amendment which would have allowed Quebec to opt out of national programs, with fiscal compensation.[4] The amendment was defeated.

The transition from CCF to NDP was accompanied by a struggle within the party to accommodate Quebec. This was expressed in the New Party Declaration on Quebec as follows:

> Our pride in Canada as a nation is enhanced by our consciousness of the two national cultures which form the basis of Canadian life. We are indeed aware that those who have their roots in the French-speaking community frequently and legitimately use the word "nation" to describe French Canada itself.

But not everyone was happy with that formulation, and Eugene Forsey, a foundation member of the CCF, walked out of the convention to protest this concession to francophones. Further schisms occurred when francophone Quebeckers, who had joined the NDP with the prospect of changing the position on the national question, eventually realized that the NDP would not budge. A particularly bitter confrontation took place in 1972, prior to the federal election campaign. Under Raymond Laliberté, the Quebec Council of the NDP adopted a program which was at variance with the Federal Council:

> The program of the Quebec NDP calls for ... political self-determination, economic self-determination, and social self-determination ... In the event of Quebec's independence, a socialist government in Ottawa, or at least a strong NDP presence, would be a valuable partner for Quebec representatives who had to negotiate the conditions of separation ... Under a real federalism, the central government has no other powers than those that are delegated by the different parts that make up the country...[5]

A news release was immediately issued by David Lewis, the federal leader, which stated in no uncertain terms:

> In its statement, the Quebec wing sets out a rather extreme concept of federalism that I cannot accept. It says: "Under real federalism, the central government has no other powers than those that are delegated by the different parts that make up the country." I cannot accept this statement. It is not and never has been NDP policy.[6]

A year later, Raymond Laliberté resigned as leader of the Quebec division of the NDP. There could be no concession between the strict centralism of the anglophone NDP leaders and the nationalism of Quebeckers, who were attracted to the NDP on social-democratic lines but were repelled by the anti-Quebec position of the party as a whole. The Wafflers in their manifesto went farther than the party, advocating the right of Quebec to self-determination, and joined in an alliance with the radical Quebeckers, which brought this rejoinder from David Lewis:

> ...the NDP-Quebec and the Waffle group must accept the policies of the Party as they are decided by the Convention ... The Party can have only one set of policies. There cannot be a policy for one province and another for all the others. Our federal candidates in Quebec must support these policies or else they cannot be candidates.[7]

But that was not always true. Lewis had tried to impose the authority of the central leadership in his various roles as National Secretary, President, and Leader, but he was only partially successful. The three provinces which had the strongest NDP organizations up to that point, and which were already electing governments — British Columbia, Saskatchewan, and Manitoba — often resisted what they called interference from the national office, and succeeded. The NDP in Quebec was not as fortunate, because it was small, had not elected anyone to public office, and above all because the anglophone majority in the NDP across Canada was hostile to the idea of Quebec being treated as "a distinct society." Moreover, this "Quebec idea" ran counter to the basic premise of the NDP and of the CCF before it, namely, that the central government must be constantly strengthened, and provincial rights made subordinate. The "Quebec idea," however, surfaced again with the Meech Lake Constitutional Accord in 1987, and set into motion a new revolt in Quebec.

This time the federal leader, Ed Broadbent, supported the Accord, which characterized Quebec as a "distinct society," and which also contained a declaration that the "Government of Canada shall provide reasonable compensation to the government of a province that chooses not to participate in a national shared-cost program ... if the province carries on a program or initiative that is compatible with the national objectives." It will be recalled that Broadbent had moved an amendment to the Charter of Rights in 1981 to include an opting out clause, but one that would be applicable only to Quebec. Howard Pawley, NDP premier of Manitoba at the time of the 1987 introduction of the Meech Lake Accord, voted with all the other first ministers to endorse its provisions, but at the leadership convention in December 1989 he reversed his position. At this same convention, Broadbent also backtracked on the Meech Lake Accord, which he had endorsed in the House of Commons. Most of the delegates, and all the candidates for the leadership, were already in opposition to the Accord, except for the sixty Quebec delegates, and some notables from anglophone Canada, such as Bob Rae and Stephen Lewis. This once again highlighted the isolation of the NDP in Quebec.

There is no doubt that one of the important reasons for the election of Phil Edmonston in the Chambly by-election, the first NDP standard-bearer in Quebec ever to win a seat in the House of Commons, was his support of Meech Lake at the NDP leadership convention. This was not the only reason, however. The disaster surrounding the explosion of the highly toxic PCB (polychlorinated biphenyl) insulators, which had occurred several years before in part of the Chambly constituency, rebounded to his benefit. He was a tireless fighter for environment control, and provided leadership to the residents who suffered catastrophic losses. Moreover, the Liberal candidate in

Chambly, Clifford Lincoln, had been Minister of the Environment in the Bourassa cabinet when this explosion took place, and he was blamed for the carelessness of the provincial government, which had neglected the minimum supervision of this site, and which had been very slow in assisting the residents in relocating while the damage was being cleaned up. The Conservative candidate was confronted with the graft and corruption that had forced the ouster of the previous incumbent, thus forcing the by-election, and as well, he was the recipient of the discontent directed at the Mulroney's record which he defended, including the Goods and Services Tax.

It was not more than two days after the NDP's stunning victory, however, when Edmonston announced that his outright support of Meech Lake did not differ from the resolution on Meech Lake that was passed at the NDP leadership convention in December. Yet all the news reports from the convention at that time said the following:

> Edmonston argued forcefully against the motion on the convention floor. He said he feared it would be perceived as "anti-Quebec" and forced him to review his decision to run for the NDP in the Chambly by-election ... Early in the campaign, Quebec party president Paul Cappon reprimanded Edmonston for defying party policy by calling for passage of the accord without changes.[8]

However, Edmonston did change his position. This significant turn made the weak position of the NDP even weaker at the open meeting of the eleven first ministers, June 23, 1990, that saw the final defeat of the Meech Lake Accord. Subsequent to that event, the NDP National Council expelled from its ranks the Quebec provincial section of the NDP, which had been attempting for several years to establish an autonomous provincial organization. The break finally came when the Quebec provincial section endorsed separatism.

The NDP is primarily an anglophone party, with the majority opposed to concessions to Quebec nationalism. This was vividly demonstrated at the party's 1989 leadership convention, as well as in the support the NDP gave Trudeau's original Charter of Rights. This position of the NDP at every juncture in federal-provincial relations has had strong support in all the provinces where the NDP is strong: in British Columbia, Saskatchewan, Manitoba, and Ontario; in the top leaderships and among the members of the Canadian Labour Congress in the same provinces; in many sections of the intellectual élite at anglophone universities, and among activists in mass movements there.

The NDP faces what appears to be an insoluable conundrum: it stands for a strong central government, whereas Quebec wants to have the strong powers and cede only the lesser jurisdictions to Ottawa. The NDP might agree to a formula which would treat Quebec as a special case, and that would probably lose a great deal of support in the other provinces, or it could agree to the separation of Quebec, with sovereign association between it and the rest of Canada. But a better option would be to try to convince English Canada to accept Quebec as a province distinct from the others.

8

The CCF-NDP in Power

Within eleven years after the foundation of the CCF, the party won five successive provincial elections in Saskatchewan between 1944 and 1960, was defeated in 1964 and 1967, won again in 1971, 1975, and 1978, and again in 1991. In 1969, the NDP became the government of Manitoba for the first time, was re-elected in 1973, defeated in 1977, then re-elected in 1981 and 1986. In 1972, the NDP was elected as the government of British Columbia, was defeated at the next election in 1975, but won the election of 1991. On September 6, 1990, the NDP won the provincial election in Ontario for the first time. Thus in four provinces the CCF-NDP has had the opportunity to enact some of its programs. But it has not yet had that opportunity at the federal level, where it remains a party of the Opposition, with all its limitations. Yet the party's leadership, including Audrey McLaughlin, who became national leader at the convention of December 1989, continued to be wedded to the idea that a strong central government is the main goal and that CCF-NDP provincial governments are of secondary importance. But it does not seem to be likely that a NDP government will be elected at the federal level in the near future, because of Quebec, and the inability of the NDP to formulate a position which can be accepted by francophone Quebeckers.

In the history of the CCF, and even during the beginnings of the NDP, one of the chief advocates of centralism was Frank Scott, who in January 1943 made this observation:

> The Regina Manifesto was basically sound. We must carry back to all parts of the movement that unless we elect a CCF government federally, the people of Canada will

not have economic security, no matter how strong our provincial movements may be.[1]

When the Saskatchewan CCF took over the reins of government in 1944, it faced a threat from the federal government to prevent a provincial act that would limit the mortgage companies from fore-closing on farms that had been hit during the depression. Under a storm of protest Mackenzie King withdrew this threat, but made it clear that he would not hesitate to use the federal government's power to disallow provincial legislation, even if the legislation was within the province's rights. Premier Douglas wrote Frank Scott, who was considered the CCF expert on constitutional matters, and suggested that the party should demand the removal of the federal power to disallow. Scott refused, stating that the "provinces should not be allowed to develop into glorified little states at the expense of the federal government." [2] But whatever Douglas may have thought about the primacy of the central government before his election as premier, he was compelled to fight for provincial rights against the federal government, and also at times within the party itself against its rigid interpretation of centralism, particularly by M. J. Coldwell, David Lewis, and Frank Scott.

At the outset, the newly-elected CCF government was faced with the lack of experience of the forty-seven CCF MLAs who had been elected for the first time as members of the ruling party. What help could they expect from the leading people of the CCF in the House of Commons or in the national office, who were just as inex-perienced? What help could they expect from the Saskatchewan civil service, most of whom were Liberals, and many of whom had been employed not for their expertise in running a province, but for their loyalty to the Liberal machine?

On the other hand, the forty-seven who had been elected on the CCF ticket and who now had to assume the awesome burden of managing the provincial affairs, represented a cross-section of the populist movements which had produced the Saskatchewan section of the CCF. They had come from the Farmer-Labour Party, the co-operatives, the Saskatchewan Grain Growers Association, the In-dependent Labour Party, and assorted socialist groups. They had lived through the Great Depression, which had hit their province harder than any other, and many had participated in the struggles which took place during that period.

Although the war was still on when the first CCF government took office, the members felt that the end of the war was in sight, and it would be their responsibility to begin the post-war reconstruction within the constitutional jurisdiction of the province. But they also had to be prepared to enter into federal-provincial negotiations to change the character of post-war Canada, and make it a more just society.

An Economic Advisory and Planning Board was set up in January 1946, which reported to the Cabinet on November 29, 1947 with a document entitled *A Four-Year Plan* which subordinated its proposals to a national plan of the CCF: [3]

> The purpose of comprehensive Socialist planning is to mobilize our communal resources, to raise the over-all standard of living and to ensure an equitable distribution of economic wealth and privilege. The CCF believes that the achievement of such a purpose can only be effected by replacing the present Capitalist system with a Socialist form of society ... To institute a true planned economy in Saskatchewan, the CCF must first capture power at Ottawa.[4]

The main theme of this report was that the CCF government would have to proceed slowly on most of its program, either until a CCF government "captured power in Ottawa," or the present federal government would enter into agreements with the provinces, sharing costs on social legislation, on the Trans-Canada highway, and on health and medicare.

> Consequently, our Four-Year Plan is hedged by a very sober recognition of provincial limitations and is based upon a realistic appraisal of the economic potential of Saskatchewan. It is not, therefore, spectacular. It is not new ...[5]

The Report was unequivocal in demanding that the federal government assume old-age pensions; that it participate and give leadership to Dominion-Provincial fiscal arrangements, and enact equalization grants to the provinces:

> The primary aim of a Social Services program is to effect a redistribution of wealth in order to ensure a decent standard of living for all. Until a redistribution is achieved ... the provinces cannot hope to provide adequate social services. It is submitted, therefore, that a hold the line policy must be adopted in the social service field until Federal aid is secured ... Because of other pressing social security obligations, Saskatchewan has little money for cultural amenities such as libraries, community centres, etc. A hold the line policy must be adopted in this field as well, and the other goals would have to be shelved, at least for the time being.[6]

A similar approach was taken on capital expenditures, such as highways, electrification, mineral exploration, and establishing crown companies in lumber, woollen mills, tanneries, buses, and printing companies. It was clear that there was little money for capital investment, and a small allocation for further study was all the Economic Advisory and Planning Board would recommend.

Labour policy, it stated, should be limited to making the existing "advanced legislation" province-wide, but the province should continue to press the federal government to take over jurisdiction on labour matters in order to achieve national minimum standards. The reason for this was puzzling, because labour legislation does not require a great outlay of money to have the province become the repository of the most advanced labour standards in the country.

The CCF victory in Saskatchewan in June 1944 had been followed by a victory in the federal elections of June, 1945, when the CCF won eighteen of Saskatchewan's twenty-one seats in the House of Commons. King displayed his hostility to the CCF government by his threat to disallow the Farm Security Act. He followed that by suspending payment by the federal government of the cash transfer it owed to Saskatchewan under the wartime tax rental agreement.[7]

This was the same prime minister who, before he was defeated in June 1930, had stated that he would never give a five-cent piece for unemployment relief to any province that elected a Conservative government. It was the same prime minister, who disallowed Alberta's Social Credit legislation in 1937 to bring about monetary reform.

The actions of the federal government against the two provincial administrations that were outside the established party system strengthened the belief, especially in the West, that these new provincial governments were battling against the monied interests of central Canada, who were served by either of the two old-line parties which alternated as the government in Ottawa.

Yet a sharp conflict developed between the Social Credit in Alberta and the CCF in Saskatchewan, the former declaring its government to be the standard-bearer of Prairie capitalism, and the latter standing unequivocally for socialism. According to a recent study of Social Credit, it went "from a reformist party opposed to the bankers to a conservative party opposed to the socialists ..." [8] On the other hand, the CCF government in Saskatchewan, while upholding its socialist doctrine, stated at the outset that it could not bring about socialism on a provincial basis, and would have to be content with carrying out reforms, and even there, it would have to proceed cautiously.

This was a far cry from the red scare that the country's leading capitalists generated in 1943:

> If Ottawa showed concern at the CCF surge, Bay Street reacted in terror. The country's leading capitalists ... formed a committee of twenty-one to battle the socialist hordes ... They rang all the bells the reactionaries had sounded in 1919, but they rang them louder. Socialism equalled Communism. The CCF would confiscate property, bank accounts, and life insurance. The left would impose a government of, by, and for the shiftless and the incompetent, and "advocates of free enterprise would be regarded as guilty of treason." [9]

This hysteria could not be justified by the campaign programs of the CCF in Ontario in 1943, or in Saskatchewan in 1944, nor in the campaign of the federal CCF in 1945. In contrast, the CCF government of Saskatchewan, for its first four-year term, hesitated to introduce in the Legislature any of the mild reforms it had promised in the 1944 election platform.

In the first place, it was compelled to oppose the federal government, particularly in the measures which Ottawa had taken against it. Douglas preferred to co-operate with King on federal-provincial fiscal arrangements in order to move gradually towards a welfare state.

Between 1944 and 1957, the main framework of the post-war federal-provincial fiscal arrangements was put in place. All provinces except Quebec would permit the federal government to collect the personal, corporation, and succession taxes, and return an agreed-upon percentage to the provinces. All provinces that would agree to federal partnership in social and health expenditures would share fifty-fifty in the costs, which would be renegotiated every five years; and a complicated system of equalization payments would average out the provincial revenues, with the richer provinces (British Columbia, Alberta, and Ontario) getting no additional payments, and the revenue of other provinces, including Quebec, being supplemented by the federal government.

There is no doubt that the presence of a CCF government during all the negotiations between the federal and provincial governments that brought about such a major alteration in federal-provincial relations, was decisive to that outcome. But Douglas could not be satisfied until old age pensions on a contributory basis, to supplement the universal old age pensions and medicare, were enacted.

Medicare was adopted by Premier T. C. Douglas as an urgent goal very shortly after he assumed political power. A report which he had commissioned from Dr. Henry Sigerst, professor of medical history at Johns Hopkins University, was ready before the end of 1944.

> The goal is clear, it must be to provide complete medical services to all the people of the province, irrespective of their economic status, and irrespective of whether they live in town or country.[10]

The urgency of a broad old age pension, over and beyond the kind which had been in existence, in one form or another, since 1927, appeared in many government documents, but primarily in the *Four-Year Plan* of November 1947. But at that time it appeared, along with medicare, as programs which had to be implemented by the federal government, or as a federal-province arrangement. Many of these programs finally became legislated realities: the Canada Pension Plan was enacted by the federal government in 1965, and approved by all the provinces except Quebec, which enacted its own plan. The Medical Care Insurance Act was passed by the Saskatchewan Legislature in 1961, and made nation-wide in 1966 as the Medical Care Act, a federal-provincial arrangement.

> Medicare was the greatest single achievement in the political career of Tommy Douglas. Perhaps more than any other event in Canadian history, the coming of state health

insurance to Saskatchewan fulfilled the hopes of the social
gospel reformers. It made high-quality health care available to everyone, regardless of their ability to pay.[11]

But more than that, medicare in Saskatchewan broke the logjam
that threatened to stop or slow down the redistribution of the nation's
wealth, and gave meaning to the changes in federal-provincial relations that had evolved out of the Rowell-Sirois Commission Report
in 1945.

It also showed how important the provinces, or in this case a single
province, can be in Canadian federalism. There is no doubt that
Mackenzie King wanted to strengthen the powers of the central
government, and that Premier Maurice Duplessis of Quebec and
Premier George Drew of Ontario vigorously opposed him. But King
was not too clear as to why he wanted these powers, except as
preventive measures against another depression. Douglas's position
was to support King, but to demand that the shift in taxation to the
federal treasury be used largely to finance the expansion of social,
health, and welfare measures that would provide state aid to cover
everybody "from the cradle to the grave." It was this position, that
won out in the end, even though the Liberal Party led successively
by Mackenzie King, Louis St. Laurent, and Lester Pearson, took the
credit for the legislation.

Beginning in the 1950s, the Canadian economy started an upward
ascent, which continued up until 1990, except for several brief reces-
sions, and a consistent lag in the economy of the Atlantic provinces.
In this new climate the Saskatchewan CCF was able to carry through
most of its platform, either as provincial legislation or as federal-provincial projects. Highlights of its provincial legislation were: labour
laws which became a model for the labour movement throughout the
country; rural electrification; development of natural resources and
the expansion of the publicly-owned telephone system; the building
of small crown corporations owning industries such as timber, tan-
nery, printing, and bus companies; larger corporations for the exploration and mining of potash, coal, and silica; aiding co-operatives in
agricultural and fish products; and building provincial highways, and
schools.

None of these were particularly controversial, although the Liberals, Conservatives, and Social Credit parties never missed an opportunity to denounce all CCF and NDP initiatives.

Besides the fierce battles that took place around medicare, the creation of government-owned automobile insurance also aroused the opposition:

> As with other innovations of the CCF government, it was under fire from all political opponents and private insurance companies on principle. In 1946, an opposition member described it "as the greatest swindle perpetrated on Saskatchewan people." [12]

Yet when the CCF-NDP was defeated in 1964, the Liberal Party, which became the government, did not make any changes either to medicare or the auto insurance law, even though they had denounced them persistently and vehemently.

The government of the CCF-NDP lost the 1964 election by 660 votes over the whole province. It received 40.3 percent of the popular vote and twenty-five seats, compared to the Liberal Party's 40.4 percent of the vote but thirty-two seats. What accounted for the Saskatchewan NDP's defeat at the zenith of its achievements?

In the 1960 election, which was fought on the issue of medicare, the CCF-NDP was returned with 276,846 votes, or 40.8 percent and thirty-seven seats, against the Liberal Party's 221,932 votes, or 31.5 percent and seventeen seats.

If the issue of medicare was the main factor in 1964 in defeating the CCF, why did the CCF win the previous election on the same issue? The difference between the CCF-NDP vote in these two elections was only 0.5 percent.

Between 1960 and 1964 two events could have accounted for this difference: the doctors' strike and the resignation of Douglas as premier and provincial leader to become national leader of the New Democratic Party.

The doctors' strike took place in the summer of 1962, after the Medical Care Insurance Act had passed the Saskatchewan Legislature in November 1961 but before it was implemented in July 1962. The strike was unsuccessful, but it created considerable turmoil and led to the personal defeat of Douglas in the Regina City riding in the federal elections that took place in June.

It was Douglas's opinion, stated in 1980, that the decision to make him the national leader of the NDP was a major factor in the 1964 defeat of the Saskatchewan party. [13]

What was the reasoning behind the decision of the federal leadership of the CCF to draft Douglas as leader of what was to be a new
party? On the surface, the reasons were obvious. Douglas was then
undoubtedly the most popular CCFer in the country, whose leadership
to the first CCF government was widely acclaimed, and whose
greatest triumph was still ahead but within sight, namely, medicare.

Was that sufficient reason to remove him from the successful
premiership of a province to lead a national party which had never
polled more than 15.6 percent of the federal electorate, as compared
to its Saskatchewan counterpart, which in the provincial arena was
from its start the second and then the first party in the Legislature?
Conceivably, the decision to make Douglas national leader was a
value judgement, comparing the relative importance of federal and
provincial politics.

But a judgement of a different order should have been made. This
had to do with Tommy Douglas's relationship with the labour movement, and especially with the top officers of the Canadian Labour
Congress, who were part of the leadership of the new party, as they
never were in the CCF. His background, as well as his aptitude, did
not lend themselves to a close relationship with the labour leaders,
nor did his relations with David Lewis, which at the beginning were
respectful and affectionate, but deteriorated after a few years in the
national leadership. When Stephen Lewis asked Douglas in 1968 to
step down, the rupture was complete, although still hidden from the
public and even from the rank-and-file of the NDP and from the trade
unions which were affiliated to it.[14]

After the defeat of the CCF-NDP in the 1964 provincial elections,
the party was headed by Woodrow Lloyd. In the 1967 election, the
NDP increased its percentage of the popular vote from 40.3 percent
in 1964 to 44.3 percent, but lost one seat, from 25 to 24. The Liberal
Party, on the other hand, increased its share of the popular vote from
40.4 percent to 45.6 percent and its seats from thirty-two to thirty-five.
But in the following election, June 23, 1971, under the leadership of
Allan Blakeney, the NDP recaptured the government with 55.0 percent of the vote, the largest percentage it had ever received, and
increased its seats to forty-five out of sixty.

But it was in many ways a different NDP. In the first place,
Saskatchewan was more prosperous. The NDP government became
a champion of provincial rights, and soon after extended the battle
cry to a defense of "the West," which included Manitoba, Alberta,
and British Columbia:

> Premier Blakeney emerged a competent champion of the
> western cause not only in election campaigns but also in
> federal-provincial conferences and in public statements.[15]

The demands of the West had changed to emphasize industriali-
zation and extraction of natural resources, against what appeared to
be federal interference. In a speech made in Toronto in January 1977,
Blakeney charged that the federal government under Trudeau had
joined with one of the big potash corporations to upset the Saskatchewan government's legitimate rights in natural resources. Ottawa, according to him, was interfering with the West's rights to
determine and collect the royalty payments on oil and potash, but did
not demand the same from Ontario's mineral production.

But this attack on the central government was contrary to the stand
of the federal NDP under David Lewis and Ed Broadbent, its two
national leaders during the Blakeney regime. They supported the
leadership of the prime minister, Pierre Trudeau, who had decided to
fight for greater powers for the federal government, and this seemed
to be in line with the basic attitude of the NDP to strengthen the
central government at all times.

Under Broadbent, the federal NDP caucus gave unqualified support to Trudeau's drive to amend the Constitution with or without the
consent of the provinces. Initially directed at Quebec, but opposed
also by seven anglophone provinces including Saskatchewan, this
struggle ended in a partial victory for Trudeau and his ally Broadbent.
It was a defeat for the province of Quebec, and a compromise with
the other anglophone premiers, most of whom insisted, as their price
for agreeing to the Charter, on the insertion in the Charter of the now
famous "notwithstanding clause" which had been drafted by Premier
Blakeney.

The schism which developed between the federal executive and
the Saskatchewan NDP demonstrated that provincial NDP parties do
not always follow the federal policies of their party, thus demonstrating that they have become part of the provincial party system, regardless of the theoretical goals of Canadian social democracy.

* * *

Winnipeg was the birthplace of the social-democratic political party
in Canada. It was the political home of J. S. Woodsworth, where he
won his first election to the House of Commons in 1921 and every
election thereafter until his death in 1942. He emerged as the out-

standing figure in the Winnipeg General Strike; the leading personal-
ity in the Independent Labour Party in Manitoba; the author of a series
of articles on the need for a social-democratic party; the honorary
president of the League for Social Reconstruction in 1932; and the
founder and first president of the Co-operative Commonwealth Federation (CCF) in 1933.

In Winnipeg he was surrounded by other labour politicians: seven
labour aldermen in the Winnipeg city council and in 1922 and 1923
a labour mayor; eleven members elected to the Manitoba Legislature
in 1920; and a new labour member of Parliament, A. A. Heaps,
elected in 1925 in North Winnipeg. Woodsworth was the main target
for attack by the ruling élite in Manitoba. He was arrested during the
General Strike; the RCMP opened a file on him upon his return to
Winnipeg on June 9, 1919, and kept it up to date for the rest of his
life.[16] The ideologue of Winnipeg's Wellington Crescent set, J. W.
Dafoe, declared that "theoretically, at any rate, the Independent
Labour Party is identified with the communist political philosophy,"
and J. S. Woodsworth was "almost mentally unbalanced with respect
to Social and Labor questions." [17]

Winnipeg was the only Canadian city in which the majority of the
population was working-class, and in which a whole area was in-
habited by poor, non-anglophone immigrants. It was also the city
which had two trade union councils: the Trades and Labour Council
(AFL) and after 1919, the One Big Union (OBU).

When the CCF was founded in Regina, 1933, the Manitoba Independent Labour Party wanted to retain its name, while being an
integral part of the new party. It took several years and the personal
intervention of Woodsworth to obtain agreement that the name would
be CCF and not ILP.[18] Another difference between the Manitoba CCF
and the National Executive erupted in 1940 as a result of an invitation
from Premier John Bracken to the seven CCF members of the
Legislature, who had been elected in 1936, to join a coalition for the
duration of the war. The national leaders opposed this, because they
failed to see the benefits and, in fact, could see only harm to the CCF.
But the CCF MLAs insisted and entered the "coalition" of the Lib-
eral-Progressive government of John Bracken, only to find a few
years later that Bracken deserted the Liberals, and what remained of
the Progressives, to become national leader of the Conservatives, after
this party added the word "Progressive" to its name. Running for the
first time as part of the Coalition, the CCF in the election of 1941,
lost four out of its seven seats.[19]

The problem for the CCF was how to expand from its Winnipeg base into the rest of the province. Starting in 1945, the CCF and later the NDP did elect Members of Parliament from outside Winnipeg, in the federal ridings of Selkirk, Springfield, Churchill, and Dauphin, although on an irregular basis. But it took thirty-six years and the provincial election of June 25, 1969, to elect a NDP government in Manitoba. That election changed the political geography of the province by elevating the NDP to the status either of the occupant or contender for power, at the expense of one of the two traditional parties. This came about as a result of the election, for the first time, of NDP standard-bearers in eleven rural ridings, and it also had a great deal to do with Ed Schreyer, who had become NDP provincial leader just before the Conservative government called an election.

In an interview in May 1990, Schreyer said that nine of the eleven rural seats that went to the NDP in the 1969 provincial election covered the territory of the two federal ridings of Selkirk and Springfield, which he had held as NDP MP prior to becoming provincial leader.[20] It should be noted, however, that the riding of Selkirk had been held for the CCF in 1945, 1949, and 1957, as well as in two by-elections of 1943 and 1954, and that the constituency of Springfield was held by the CCF in 1957 by Jacob Schulz, who was president of the Farmers' Union, and later, father-in-law of Schreyer.

The greatest support the CCF or NDP had ever received in a Manitoba provincial election before 1969 was 75,333 votes, or 23.1 percent, and eleven seats in the 1966 election. The growth in NDP popularity after that can be seen in the table below:

Voting Record of Manitoba Provincial NDP Since 1969

Year	Votes	%	Seats	Status
1969	128,080 votes	38.3 %	29 seats of 57.	(Government)
1973	197,585 "	42.3 %	31 " " "	(Government)
1977	188,124 "	38.6 %	23 " " "	(Opposition)
1981	228,784 "	47.4 %	34 " " "	(Government)
1986	198,261 "	41.5 %	30 " " "	(Government)
1988	126,954 "	23.6 %	12 " " "	(Third Party)
1990	168,757 "	33.7 %	20 " " "	(Opposition)

The NDP's victory was more than a change in status: it was a change in the times, and in the generations. The last of the pioneers to occupy the national leadership was David Lewis, who had assumed that position in 1971 and for health reasons retired in 1975. With Ed Broadbent as leader in charge of the federal party, and Ed Schreyer, Allan Blakeney, and David Barrett, as NDP premiers of Manitoba,

Saskatchewan, and British Columbia, the preoccupation of the NDP and its emphases underwent a drastic change at both federal and provincial levels. In the House of Commons, Broadbent was becoming a close ally of Trudeau in his efforts to change the Constitution, and to strengthen the central government. The three provincial premiers, especially Blakeney, were much closer to Peter Lougheed, Tory premier of Alberta, in defending what they considered to be the provincial rights of the West, than they were to Trudeau or Broadbent.

Because the Manitoba NDP leadership convention was a hurried affair, Schreyer had very little time to outline his ideas, but there was no doubt that the delegates recognized the differences between him and the other contenders, and voted accordingly. He was from the rural area of Manitoba, which meant that, prior to becoming the leader of the provincial party, he had not been close to the decision-making and ideological centre of the ILP, CCF, or NDP. He referred to the provincial membership under his leadership as "a coalition." It meant, as it became clear, to drop references to socialism, or even to social democracy, in favour of stressing a pragmatic platform that could and would attract liberals, rural populists, workers, as well as social democrats.

Most of the twenty-nine MLAs on his side were professionals; there were more Catholics, including Schreyer, than ever before; there was an ethnic representation that more accurately reflected the population of the province; and there was less commitment to the socialist or even the social-democratic ideology than in any previous CCF or NDP caucus in the Manitoba Legislature.[21] This was, in differing degrees, what was happening to the NDP MPs and MLAs throughout the country. But it was particularly the case where the NDP had succeeded, to use a phrase borrowed from the first CCF government in Canada, in "capturing power," in contrast to those CCF or NDP parliamentary groups which were in opposition.

Schreyer remained premier for two terms, and was defeated by the Conservatives in the 1977 elections. The NDP, under Howard Pawley, re-captured power in 1981

The 1981 victory for the Manitoba NDP was its most resounding: 228,784 votes, or 47.4 percent and thirty-four seats. It was a straight fight between the NDP and the Conservatives and appeared, at that time, to have wiped out the Liberals, who, for the first time in the history of Manitoba, did not elect a single member. The NDP success was repeated in the 1986 elections, even though its overall vote dropped to 41.5 percent and its representation to thirty seats. But two years later, this government lost a confidence vote in the Legislature and was defeated in the subsequent election on April 26, 1988, dropping its popular vote by almost half, and its seats by more than that. Its losses allowed the Conservatives to form a minority government, even though they dropped from twenty-six to twenty-five seats. The anti-NDP sweep mainly benefited a resurgent Liberal Party, which was reborn and ready to take over as the official opposition, with twenty seats to the NDP's twelve.

The long period of NDP rule in Manitoba, from 1969 to 1977 and from 1981 to 1988, produced an impressive legislative record, highlighted by public auto insurance, abolition of medicare premiums, increased health care benefits, reformed labour codes, a freedom of information act, and the best human rights code in the country.

One of the most difficult problems for the NDP government was its support for the restoration of bilingualism to Manitoba.

In a 1985 judgement, the Supreme Court had ordered the Manitoba government to translate all legislative enactments since 1890 into French, regardless of cost. This would bring the Legislature into conformity with Article 23 of The Manitoba Act of 1870, which had called for the use of French and English in the Legislature, courts, and provincial laws, and which the English majority in the Legislature had illegally discarded in 1890.

In 1983, the Pawley government introduced a measure conforming to the provisions of the original Manitoba Act, and to provide some additional services to Franco-Manitobans in their language. The reaction against this was intense, stirred up by the Conservatives, who resorted to a procedural device that prevented the Legislature from meeting, and this finally forced the government to abandon the project.

When the Supreme Court handed down its 1985 judgement, an anti-French movement calling itself Manitoba Grassroots went into action immediately, accusing the government, and particularly the attorney-general, Roland Penner, of using the Supreme Court to impose a complete program of French services throughout the province.

The Supreme Court had confined itself to the questions it was directed to answer, but it also dealt, philosophically, with the relation between language and "human existence, development, and dignity":

> Section 23 of the *Manitoba Act, 1870* is a specific manifestation of the general right of Franco-Manitobans to use their own language ... The constitutional entrenchment of a duty on the Manitoba Legislature to enact, print and

publish in both French and English ... confers upon the judiciary the responsibility of protecting the correlative language rights of all Manitobans including the Franco-Manitoban minority.[22]

This served to arouse the opponents of bilingualism even more. They demanded an assurance from the Manitoba government that in carrying out the judgement of the Supreme Court it would not attempt to install bilingualism in "provincial services, municipal services, School Board services, provincial crown corporations, hydro, telephone, autopac ..."[23]

In the election of March 18, 1986, notwithstanding a growing backlash against francophone rights, the NDP was re-elected, although with a substantial drop from 47.4 percent to 41.5 percent in votes, and from thirty-four to thirty in seats. But there was a growing rift within the caucus over bilingualism and this became more evident over the support of Premier Pawley and Attorney-General Penner for the Meech Lake Accord, which they had agreed to in June 1987, together with all the other premiers and the prime minister.

But it was not the issue of bilingualism that essentially brought down the NDP in 1988. Its decision to raise premiums for automobile insurance and sharply increase taxes, and the subsequent defection of a member of the caucus, which put the government into a minority, resulting in its defeat in the Legislature.

The NDP was badly defeated in the 1988 election, dropping from 41.5 percent to 23.6 percent of the popular vote, and from thirty seats to twelve. However, it started to recover in 1990, with 33.7 percent of the vote, and twenty seats, which made it once more the official opposition, with the prospect of becoming the government. Nevertheless, support for the Liberals in the 1988 election in Manitoba resurrected the three-party system in provincial elections, which exists now in three legislatures, Manitoba, Ontario, and British Columbia, and in the House of Commons.

Howard Pawley said that the NDP has had no difficulty over the years in arriving at positions which would place it to the left of the Liberals or Tories, but differences did emerge within the NDP on such issues as Meech Lake, bilingualism, the status of Quebec, native rights, and abortion, which could not easily be classified as left or centre.[24] The actual defeat in the Legislature in 1988, however, was due to the defection of one NDP member on the two economic issues: auto insurance rates and increased taxes, and a decision by the premier to call for a vote on the budget after he had lost the one vote which he needed for a majority.

* * *

Although the NDP had been in provincial power in British Columbia for one period of thirty-nine months, it has been in many ways the stronghold of the party in Canada. With few exceptions, the British Columbia NDP has elected the party's largest bloc of MPs successively, in absolute and relative numbers, in the House of Commons. Provincially it has increased its vote, and in October 1991 became the government, after sixteen years in opposition.

Vote Results in B.C. Provincial Elections

1972					1975			
NDP	448,260	39.6%	38	seats	S.C.	635,482	49.2%	35 seat
S.C.	352,776	31.2%	10	"	NDP	505,396	39.2%	18 "
Lib.	185,640	20.2%	5	"	Lib.	93,379	7.2%	1 "
P.C.	143,450	12.7%	2	"	P.C.	49,796	3.9%	1 "
			55					55

1979					1983			
S.C.	677,607	48.2%	3	"	S.C.	820,807	49.8%	35 "
NDP	644,184	46.0%	26	"	NDP	741,354	44.9%	22 "
Lib.	6,662	.5%	0		Lib.	44,442	2.7%	0 "
P.C.	71,078	5.1%	0		P.C.	19,131	1.2%	0 "
			57					57

1986					1991			
S.C.	954,516	49.3%	47	"	NDP	567,696	41.2%	31 "
NDP	824,544	42.6%	22	"	Lib.	485,396	35.2%	17 "
Lib.	130,505	6.7%	0		S.C.	325,108	23.5%	7 "
P.C.	14,074	.7%	0					75
			69					

Federal, provincial, and municipal politics in British Columbia have reflected the conflict between the owners of capital wealth and the workers more consistently and more sharply than in any other province.[25] There has always been socialist representation in the Legislature in this century, and with the onset of the Great Depression, and the birth of the Co-operative Commonwealth Federation (CCF), the socialist bloc became the real opposition.

The response of the established parties was to unite against the CCF, and from 1945 through two elections to 1952 the Liberals and the Conservatives were united in a coalition government blocking the CCF. From 1952 on, the real conflict was between the new Social Credit party and the CCF-NDP. After the defeat of the NDP government in 1975, and the victory of Social Credit, the Liberals and Conservatives vacated provincial politics by agreement, in order to prevent future NDP victories in the provincial arena.

The ideology of the three anti-socialist parties was focused on the slogan of self-preservation in face of the "socialist hordes." Because the British Columbia economy was heavily based on primary extraction, such as lumber, metal mining, coal, and fish, the interest of the British Columbia capitalists — as they saw it — demanded a free hand, unhampered by government or labour, and until the CCF-NDP appeared on the scene they had been able to function very closely to this pattern.[26]

The move toward having only one capitalist party in provincial politics was spearheaded by John Ellis, British Columbia head of the Bank of Montreal, who arranged a series of dinners in the summer of 1974, at which he outlined this strategy:

> I think that by now a majority of people agree that the three parties simply must come together in order to have only one Right Wing candidate opposing the Socialists for each seat in the next election.[27]

This worked in the provincial political field until 1991, yet in every election since 1975 the NDP has increased its aggregate vote. The Social Credit party, its only opponent, has been enmeshed for some time in internal crises, often involving personal integrity among cabinet members, and these internecine battles strengthened the support for the NDP. The present situation bears out the prediction which Ellis himself had made in 1974:

> The formation of a single or unity party makes it inevitable that at a future date — five, ten, or fifteen years hence — the NDP will again be elected, being the only alternative to the proposed united party.[28]

The victory of the British Columbia NDP in 1972 was a surprise because it had been on the verge of winning in every election since

1952, only to be regularly defeated by its arch enemy, Social Credit. That victory in British Columbia was helped by the success of the NDP in Manitoba in 1969 and Saskatchewan in 1971. The major factor, however, was undoubtedly the general malaise that had set in around the British Columbia Social Credit government and especially its aged premier, W. A. C. Bennett. This resulted in a small resurgence in Liberal support (185,640 and five seats) and in support for the Progressive Conservatives (143,450 and two seats).

The road ahead for the NDP turned out to be rocky from day one. All the forces that the establishment could command were brought into play — the media, the three parties now in opposition, many powerful organizations — to persuade the people of British Columbia that the red hordes had captured power and were on the verge of turning their province into a socialist if not a Soviet republic. Yet with all the propaganda, the NDP vote in 1975 was only 0.4 percent less than it received in the previous election, which it had won. Moreover, the NDP actually increased its vote from 448,260, when it won the election, to 505,396 when it lost.

A day to day record of the British Columbia NDP, which the authors chose to call "the Dave Barrett regime," was published in 1978, with a very detailed, albeit somewhat biased, chronicle of every action of this government, under the title *The 1200 Days – A Shattered Dream.*[29] What emerges is a huge volume of legislative enactments, as well as continuous reorganizations of the government and the civil service. Unfortunately, the authors give all the legislation equal weight and importance. Yet while the NDP government grew out of a strong socialist background, none of its achievements in power could be called socialist, but rather were democratic reforms.

On the other hand, the radical left in British Columbia was ready to denounce the Barrett government even before it was installed, and continued its criticism throughout the government's tenure of office and after. A well-known Marxist professor at the University of British Columbia, in an analysis published in 1977, wrote:

> ...the NDP preferred the line of least resistance, seeking to make capitalism more livable through social expenditures, rather than attacking head on. Social expenditures however commendable, e.g. for old age supplements or day-care centres or education, do not in themselves change the material relations of production or people's political

consciousness. But, then, social democracy is not Marxism.[30]

During its three years in office, the NDP government passed 367
bills, "more than double those of the preceding three years." The most
significant of these were the Land Commission Act; the Human
Rights Code; Pharmacare, which provided free prescriptions for
seniors; Mincome, which increased the income to pensioners; laws to
assist the tenants; public auto insurance; a new and improved labour
code; and the acquisition of some of the mineral extracting and forest
companies, which it then operated as crown corporations.[31]

The laws passed by the British Columbia NDP government improved the material, and in many cases, moral well-being of the
people. Yet they all were attacked by the three opposition parties, and
by the media.

What was unusual, however, was the attack on the Labour Code
by the British Columbia Federation of Labour, which had supported
the government up to that point.[32] This attack had more to do with
philosophy than with the actual provisions of the code. Labour, and
particularly the B.C. Federation of Labour, regarded the NDP as the
labour party and therefore expected special treatment, especially in
the preparation of the Labour Code. But the Federation went further.
It insisted that the bill it would submit should be endorsed by the
government without any changes.[33]

But this was not the opinion of all the leaders of the Federation.
Foremost among the dissidents was Jack Munro, who had become
Canadian president of the International Woodworkers of America,
and who differed from the Federation:

> My biggest beef with the Federation at that time, was that
> they treated the NDP as though it were the arm of
> labour...Guy and Johnston (at that time the principal of-
> ficers of the BCFL) had this crazy notion that because the
> NDP was the government, it was there to do the bidding
> of organized labour. I think that the labour movement
> made a big mistake thinking this would be the case.[34]

The British Columbia NDP of 1972 was in many ways a different
party from the previous socialist, or CCF, and even earlier NDP. It
kept its base in the working class, but it had expanded and had drawn
support from teachers, academics, social workers, and government

employees, and this was reflected in the leadership, in the legislative caucus, and consequently in its program.

When the Labour Code was introduced in the Legislature on October 1, 1973, it was denounced by the main leadership of the B.C. Federation of Labour, and later by a majority of delegates at a convention of the New Democratic Party. But Premier Barrett and his labour minister, William King, firmly defended the code's provisions, and regarded it as a major improvement in British Columbia labour-management relations. The transfer of most labour conflicts from the courts to the jurisdiction of the Labour Board was considered as the code's main achievement, but it was brushed aside by many leaders of the Federation.

At issue in the debates within the left was the relationship between the NDP government and the NDP itself, and between the government and the B.C. Federation of Labour. Was the NDP government authoritarian in the Legislature, or did it consult the party, and the labour federation? This dilemma was compounded by the fact that the NDP leader was also the premier of the province, bound by the oath of allegiance to a different set of rules and laws. Moreover, as premier, he had to seek a consensus beyond the 39.6 percent who had voted for the NDP, and satisfy, to the best of his ability, the people who did not vote for the NDP. The reluctance of Barrett and King to accept the B.C. Federation's labour code did dampen the enthusiasm of many trade unionists in the campaign of December, 1975, even if it did not cause a decrease in the labour vote.

No matter what legislation the NDP carried out while in office, it faced a torrent of abuse by the media, which was controlled by the same monied interests that also financed the anti-socialist political parties. In Canada, with the founding of the CCF, there has been only one occasion when a daily paper supported the CCF or NDP during an election.

There is no doubt that the Barrett government was affected adversely by this constant barrage, yet the British Columbia NDP has continued to increase its popular support in every election since its defeat in 1975.

One reason for the defeat of the Barrett regime was Barrett's insistence in calling his party and his government "socialist," without explaining what was socialist about its legislative program. To avoid that, Mike Harcourt, leader of the British Columbia NDP in 1991, has already declared that "I am not a socialist" but rather "a social democrat." [35]

This is not likely to deter the anti-NDP propagandists, who will continue to denounce it as a socialist party, but this failed in the British Columbia provincial election of October 17, 1991 when the NDP under Harcourt won a decisive victory against the Social Credit, which by then had become exposed as a corrupt and reactionary party.

* * *

The victory of the Ontario NDP in the provincial elections of September 6, 1990 ended the fifty years of defeat which it and its predecessor, the CCF, had endured since it first entered provincial politics in 1937. In the 1987 election, the NDP received close to one million votes, or 26 percent of the total, and won nineteen seats. In the following election it increased its vote by five hundred thousand, close to 38 percent of the total, and seventy-four seats. In the fifty-six ridings which were won by the Liberals and Conservatives, the NDP came second in thirty-six, and in eight of these the margin was less than one thousand. The fifty-five new seats it gained in this election were for the most part in regions it had never before won.

Thus the election increased the NDP's popular support by over half a million votes, and with the new seats it was now representative of every region, and could and did claim for the first time to be a provincial party.

The reasons for this sudden and surprising turnabout are complex. The last poll taken in July 1990, *before* David Peterson had announced an election, indicated a fifty percent approval for the Liberals. Ever since the three-party system became effective in Ontario provincial politics in 1943, no party had ever polled that high a percentage of the popular vote. But a week after the election was called, Liberal support dropped drastically and never recovered, ending the campaign with 32.6 percent for what had been the governing party for only two short terms. The Progressive Conservatives, after forty-two years in power, began to lose their grip in 1985, collapsed in 1987, with 24.7 percent of the vote and sixteen seats, and again in 1990 with 23.5 percent and twenty seats.

The NDP was the beneficiary of the change in the political climate which took place between the calling of the election and voting day. The increase in popular vote was almost equal to the Liberal Party loss. The defeat of David Peterson in his own riding, which had been regarded as his invincible fortress, demonstrated that he was the main cause of his party's defeat. The voters rejected the reason he gave for calling an election after only three years and suspected it as a manoeuvre.

Many important issues emerged by the time the campaign was in high gear: Meech Lake, native rights, public auto insurance, the minimum wage, pay and job equity, a change in the landlord-tenant relationship, and the projected new federal sales tax. Peterson lost support not only because he supported the Meech Lake proposals, but because of the key role he appeared to have played at the final conference of first ministers.

The Progressive Conservatives in Ontario were able to fashion their own platform on social programs, which was an important ingredient in their long regime from 1943 to 1985. When William Davis retired in the winter of 1985, Frank Miller, the new leader, discarded this platform, turned to the right and emerged from his first campaign with fifty-two seats, as compared to the Liberals' forty-eight seats and the NDP's twenty-five. The way was clear: the Liberals and NDP signed an accord based on continuing and expanding the social program which had become a basic ingredient in Ontario politics. They also agreed that the NDP would refrain for two years from moving or supporting a motion of no confidence, and in return the Liberals would pass social legislation which had been mutually agreed upon.

There was some unease, in fact opposition, in NDP ranks regarding this accord, on the grounds that it would boost the Liberal Party at the expense of the NDP. This anxiety seemed to be confirmed when the Liberals emerged from the election of 1987 with ninety-five seats, compared to their previous forty-eight seats.

Donald C. MacDonald, a prominent figure in the NDP, and a former Ontario leader, defended the strategy of Bob Rae in his political memoirs:

> Once the Liberals escaped the commitment of the Accord, which imposed upon them a left-of-centre posture with which much of their traditional constituency is uncomfortable, they gradually reverted to Ontario's more cautious conservatism.[36]

Peterson began to break away from the reforms that had become the hallmark of the accord, and there is no doubt that this helped turn Liberal voters over to the NDP in the 1990 campaign. The NDP leaders reacted by presenting as their main thrust an expanded social reform program called "An Agenda for People," which they never thought they would be called upon to implement.

This program was announced in August, but by election day it had become clear that the economy had taken a nose-dive. Nevertheless, the NDP declared that regardless of the extent and scope of the recession, they would fulfill their promises. When its first budget was presented to the Legislature, April 29, 1991, the government of Bob Rae had decided to carry through its program, projecting a deficit of $9.7 billion.

In the short period since the NDP government took office, it has faced an unprecedented onslaught, even before it had presented its major bills. In fact, the opposition parties at times have even challenged the government's right to legislate. For the first time in Ontario's political history, the executives of Bay Street, who are within a stone's throw of Queen's Park, marched on the legislative building with banners, noise-makers, megaphones, and assorted paraphernalia to protest against the government's decision not to cut social and other progressive measures in face of the recession.

The election of an NDP government in the largest and most industrialized province in the country, and with a solid majority of seats, was devastating to the corporate élite, who had enjoyed a cosy relationship with the Conservative governments for forty-two years, and were developing a similar relationship with the Liberals. They are now faced with a different type of party, which is ready to be amenable, but not at the expense of the ordinary people.

* * *

The CCF at its beginning declared its adherence to two fundamental principles: "the eradication of capitalism" and a strong central government. J. S. Woodsworth declared many times that the two were not incompatible. He advocated a strengthening of the present powers of the central government, even though it was a capitalist government. But he also asserted that there was no possibility of building socialism or "the co-operative commonwealth," except through the federal government. He stated this as doctrine, clearly and unequivocally, in the famous debate he launched in the House of Commons in February 1933. In the resolution with which he opened the debate, he moved that the Conservative government of R. B. Bennett should immediately take measures to set up a co-operative commonwealth,

in which all natural resources and the socially necessary
machinery of production will be used in the interests of
the people and not for the benefit of the few.[37]

In other words, socialism could be brought in by a Conservative
or Liberal party, but it could only be done in the House of Commons
by the government of the day. Woodsworth knew that no capitalist
party would agree to that, and therefore it would have to be the CCF
that would usher in the socialist commonwealth.

In the almost sixty years since that party and its successor have
been in existence, the co-operative commonwealth has not been realized, but the CCF and the NDP have been able to form governments
in four provinces, and by reason of their strength in those provinces,
exercise national influence through Canada's federal-provincial division of powers, and the federal-provincial fiscal arrangements.

This evolution has changed the NDP considerably. The annual
federal convention no longer has the importance within the party it
had, although it now probably has more media coverage by reason of
the fact that it is the third party on the federal level. The NDP won
forty-three seats in the House of Commons in the 1988 general election and one in a subsequent by-election, giving it the largest number
it has ever had.

The provincial parties, especially in Saskatchewan, Manitoba,
British Columbia, and Ontario, are autonomous, and often adopt
important political positions at variance with the others, including the
federal party.

Socialism, democratic socialism, social democracy, and secular
socialism, — all of which are used to describe the ideology of the
NDP — do not appear in the election platforms or even in the convention resolutions. They are, however, used with careless abandon
by the enemies of the NDP to intimidate the voters. When David
Peterson understood that he was losing the election to the NDP, he
resorted to this strategy. It did not work. It probably backfired, since
he could not explain how he was able to hold power by forming an
alliance with the socialist "troops" of the NDP in 1985.

9

Socialism Then and Now

> Our ultimate object must be a complete turnover in the
> present economic and social system. In this we recognize
> our solidarity with the workers the world over ... We must
> attack the enemy all along the line, using both political
> and industrial power, and any other legitimate power at
> our disposal.
>
> — J. S. Woodsworth, 1919 [1]

James Shaver Woodsworth, the founder of the social-democratic
party in Canada, differentiated between socialism through evolution, and Marxism, which was already being held up by the nascent
communist parties as the banner of the Russian Revolution, and the
only proven path to socialism. Socialism by evolution, or socialism
by revolution, appeared then to be merely a difference in tactics. But
it soon became clear that building a socialist society by democratic
means separated social democracy or Fabianism from the Russian
model in every way.

In the last decade of the twentieth century, communist parties and
regimes have practically disappeared from most countries: in Eastern
Europe and what used to be the Soviet Union, and in democratic
countries like Canada, where communism had run its course.

Social democracy today is a vibrant and meaningful force in
Canada, even though the founders of the CCF-NDP had pictured its
development differently. They had insisted that to "eradicate capitalism," the social-democratic party would have to capture power at the
centre, and therefore its main attention would be on federal elections
and a strong federal party. But so far, the CCF and NDP have been
successful in forming governments in four provinces, which, because

of provincial jurisdictions, have been limited in what they could achieve.

Bob Rae, in a speech given on January 10, 1990, went beyond the traditional differences in the socialist idea as they have been understood. According to him, Marxism and Fabianism were both wrong:

> ... two kinds of socialists, Marxists and Fabians, have attempted to impose the rigid view that whether by violent revolution or peaceful evolution, socialism of some kind was inevitable.[2]

Marxism was wrong, according to Rae, because it was based on the thesis that the working class would become more and more "impoverished" under capitalism, and thereby would be driven to overthrow the capitalist system and establish socialism. But with the rise of trade unions "the working class concentrated its efforts ... on improving wages and working conditions and have been remarkably successful."[3]

> Even those earnest and determined Fabians like Beatrice and Sydney Webb wrote earnestly of the "inevitability of gradualness," and the logical evolution of the modern industrial state into a socialist commonwealth. This widely shared optimism about how modern democratic socialism would come to be, has been shattered by many different forces.[4]

The Co-operative Commonwealth Federation, the Regina Manifesto, and the speeches of Woodsworth at the founding convention in 1933, were unmistakably the Canadian prototype of Fabianism.

Does the NDP still believe in the type of socialism that was adopted in 1933 by the CCF? According to its official documents, the answer would have to be in the affirmative.

The aim of the Co-operative Commonwealth Federation was summed up in the last paragraph of the Regina Manifesto:

> No CCF Government will rest content until it has eradicated capitalism and put into operation the full programme of socialized planning which will lead to the establishment in Canada of the Co-operative Commonwealth.

At its national convention in Regina, July 1983, the New Democratic Party, celebrating the fiftieth anniversary of the Regina Manifesto, adopted "A New NDP Statement of Principles" which declared in the last paragraph:

> The New Democratic Party will not rest content until we have achieved a democratic socialist Canada, and we are confident that only such a Canada can make its rightful contribution to a more just, democratic and peaceful world.

Nevertheless, there were differences between this Statement and the Regina Manifesto. There was now a recognition of the greater role of the provinces in the Canadian federation. Socialists still believe that social ownership is an essential means to achieve our goals but nationalization will be used only in "the transfer of title of large enterprises to the state."

But the 1983 Statement acknowledged that the Regina Manifesto "underestimated" the nationalist feelings of the Québécois and that "we in the NDP assert the right of the Québécois to determine their own future, but we hope that in the exercise of their democratic rights they do not choose independence." Recognition of aboriginal rights, women's rights, and the vital importance of the protection of the environment were included and reflected more accurately the views of contemporary Canadians.

None of these changes conflict with the basic aims of the NDP or the CCF:

> Socialists believe in planning. We reject the capitalist theory that the unregulated laws of supply and demand should control the destiny of society and its members ... Canadians want a strong Canadian government, strong enough to guarantee our national independence and our ability to force a strong Canadian economy in the face of world competition.

Yet criticism has developed among some members and supporters of the NDP, as exemplified by two books that have appeared in 1991 on the future of the NDP and its program: *Social Democracy Without Illusions* and *Debating Canada's Future*.[5] But this criticism, coming mainly but not exclusively from academics, bears no resemblance to previous criticism from within the NDP, such as the Waffle, or left caucuses.

Allan Blakeney, one-time NDP premier of Saskatchewan, in his essay in the first of these books, offers three main items which he wants the NDP to adopt:

> ... I want Canada to minimize reliance on the protectionist option. Social democrats must guard against a mindless defence of all manufacturing jobs ... We Canadians need a more positive attitude toward technological change — the getting rid of obsolete technologies — even when it means factory closures.[6]

Henry Milner accuses the NDP of being irresponsible, of having

> never given much attention to the day-to-day requirements of a social democratic society ... One such requirement is the need to pay for generous social programs and income redistribution. In order to gain (probably fleeting) popular approval, NDPers gleefully jumped on the bandwagon against the federal goods and services tax (GST), giving little heed to the dangers of fomenting a tax revolt that erodes popular willingness to fund redistributive programs.[7]

Milner proposes a new Regina Manifesto for the 1990s, which must be written "as if there were no NDP candidates to elect, no CLC bureaucrats to reconcile, no feminist, ecological, or other progressive interest group to appease with the correct choice of language."[8] It must abandon the concept of a planned economy, which never worked. It must embrace the free market system, it must encourage managers of firms to "maximize profit."

> To be blunt, in our new manifesto we must not only be prepared to live with capitalism; we should welcome it where it contributes to the real wealth of the community.[9]

John McCallum, chair of the Economics department at McGill, calls his piece "Confessions of a One-Time NDPer," in which he explains why "I cannot take that party seriously."

He argues against the concept that collective bargaining is an untouchable, because a sound monetary policy must be combined with a direct control on wages. He is opposed to deficit budgets, to universality in social programs, and government-provided child care. He supports the GST, but would include food as taxable. He is enthusiastic about the U.S.-Canada Free Trade Agreement.[10] In other words, he is opposed to the present and, by inference, the past programs and platforms of the CCF-NDP. His own program is not much different from that of the Mulroney government. His views hardly qualify as part of the concepts and political space of social democracy, as they have been understood, or put into the title as "Social Democracy Without Illusions."

The other volume, *Debating Canada's Future* has the sub-title "Views From the Left," and contains differing opinions on a number of topics. Not all the essays are left-wing, however, at least by current understanding of that term.

Many of the writers in these two publications, who advocate sweeping changes in Canadian social-democratic thought and practice, inevitably raise in the minds of the readers the question of whether the authors are suggesting that the NDP has become obsolete.

An essay by Henry and Arthur Milner, in *Debating Canada's Future*, attempts to circumvent this basic question by declaring that they distinguish between democratic socialism, which they oppose, and social democracy, which they favour. Democratic socialism, they argue, stands for public ownership as the preferred weapon in the fight to advance the cause of socialism, whereas social democracy does not. Democratic socialism supports all trade union demands, including "the protection of every job and industry, no matter how inefficient ..." but social democracy draws the line at some of the trade union demands.[11]

Socialism developed during this century as an ideology, a theory, and a movement, existing in most countries. In 1917, the Bolshevik faction of the Russian Social-Democratic Labour Party, seized power, changed its name to the Communist Party, formed a Communist International, and declared that their main struggle would be to destroy social democracy. But seventy-five years later, the Soviet Union finally collapsed after it had been revealed, at home and abroad, to be not a socialist country, but a brutal bureaucratic command system based on compulsory labour, either in low-paid jobs or as slave labour in gulags, with the party bureaucrats in control.

The struggle between communist and social-democratic parties led directly to the victory of fascism in Italy and Germany. In Canada, the most telling effect was felt in the trade union movement, where the battle between communists and CCFers impeded the drive to organize the unorganized, and for a period, blocked the effort to bring trade unions into political action.

In most of the democratic countries the social-democratic parties forged ahead of the communists, particularly because the latter denied the brutalities in the Soviet Union and its satellites. On the other hand, social-democratic parties in Sweden, Britain, Greece, France, Australia, New Zealand, Spain, and Portugal, became on different occasions the governments in these countries, but did not "capture power." They saw their role as managers of a market economy, who tried and succeeded to a greater or lesser extent in bringing about reforms to benefit the middle class, the workers, and farmers. The welfare state, beginning in Britain in 1946 under the Labour government, was fought for and implemented in most of the countries of western Europe, and as a result improved the living conditions of the people.

The CCF and NDP have not been elected as a government at the federal level, but have formed four provincial governments. Through their strength in these four provinces, they have succeeded in bringing about social reforms, which have been copied by other provinces, and particularly have formed federal and federal-provincial programs, such as medicare, which have set an example internationally. They have now given the lead to a Canadian Social Charter as indispensable to any revision of the Canadian Constitution.

These social programs served two purposes: they raised the living standards of society, and by so doing, made available additional purchasing power. In turn, this has been an important factor in the phenomenal increase in the production of consumer goods, which in turn stimulated industrial growth and employment. These programs, and especially the principle of universality, are supported by the majority of Canadians, and by the NDP, but are not given the same priority by the other parties in Parliament.

Social democracy was developed in Canada from the end of the last century, mainly by working-class immigrants from Europe. Marxism was part of that development, and a component of the social-democratic movement. An article in the *Canadian Magazine* of August, 1894, entitled "Canadian Democracy and Socialism" claimed:

> Karl Marx (1818-1883) is the author of the famous book "Capital" — the Bible of social democrats, which has now great influence in the United States and Canada.[12]

After the Russian Revolution, the conflict between the communists and socialists grew in bitterness all over the world. The communists claimed that they were the true Marxists and socialists, having merged the theories of Marx with those that came out of the Russian Revolution and its leader, Lenin. Marxism-Leninism was the new dogma; but Marx and Lenin were replaced by Stalin, whose catechism, *The Foundations of Leninism*, became compulsory reading among Communists, in the Soviet Union and elsewhere.

Marxism was tainted in the social-democratic lexicon because the communists had appropriated it, and equated it with the "dictatorship of the proletariat." A book on the Canadian economy, *Social Planning for Canada*, published in 1935 by the League for Social Reconstruction, a movement very close to the CCF, does not mention Marx, even though it had used much of his critique of capitalist economy.[13]

It was not until the late 1960s that the study and teaching of Marx's writings became more widely acceptable in Canada, particularly at universities and colleges, by young academics — students and professors — as was happening in Europe and in the United States. An article in *Saturday Night*, September 1979, entitled "Karl Marx Comes to Canada" made this comment:

> You can't make a precise count of Canadian academics who are Marxists or are informed by the Marxist tradition, but there are at least 300 of them, mainly in the political science and sociology departments. (A generation ago there were a few dozen.) They are among the best and brightest and the busiest.

Just at the time this article was published, a similar one appeared in the *Queen's Quarterly*, by Terry Morley, an NDP professor, called "Canada and the Romantic Left."[14] Morley added two other disciplines — Canadian labour history and general history — to the already sizable list in which the Marxist "romantics," as he called them, were making inroads. They were advancing, according to him, because "these socialists have in common an ornate and more exciting vision of the good life and a better world than do the acknowledged leaders of the socialist forces in Canada in the New Democratic Party and the trade union movement." The author then dismisses the new Marxism as a made-up replica of the old.

But the new Marxism is not a repetition of the old. It studies all aspects of Marx's analysis and tries to apply them or to revise them from today's viewpoint. They attest to the continued popularity of Marx, and by their works, are adding to it.

The new Marxism has very little to do with revolutionary politics, and even less with the Soviet Union or other communist countries. Political activity for the Marxist academic is most likely in the NDP.

But parliamentary activity is not, and never has been, the only channel for political activity: the former is restricted to parties; the latter to mass movements. Socialists, whether social-democrats or communists, have made use of mass movements, particularly trade unions, to exert pressure on parliaments, legislatures, and municipalities, and often to create new political demands.

Mass movements outside the trade union congresses have become a more powerful and more successful means of political pressure than ever before. The revolt of the Afro-Americans for their civil rights in the United States was followed closely by widespread resistance to the Vietnam War. These successful movements helped spark other movements, on such issues as nuclear disarmament, against U.S. domination of Canada, the world-wide crusade against apartheid in South Africa, solidarity with the Sandanistas in Nicaragua, and the struggle for the rights of the aboriginal people in Canada.

Amidst these events, the women's movement, one of the most important developments in this century, came to the fore and transformed the character of women's demands, and the consciousness of millions of women and men. It is not accidental that the four NDP governments in Canada have the largest number of women cabinet ministers of all the parties, and is the only one which has a woman, Audrey McLaughlin, as national leader.

The environmental movement is another powerful peoples' movement which is accelerating and which has already influenced people and legislative institutions on an international scale.

None of these movements was initiated by social-democratic parties, but the demands have been accepted and absorbed into the platforms of most social-democratic parties, including the NDP, and as a result have changed their outlook and public image. Social democracy has now gone beyond the fight for economic and social goals, and embraces far wider concerns.

But what about the goal of socialism, which distinguishes a social-democratic party from other parliamentary parties in a capitalist democracy? What about the planned economy which the NDP still holds as essential to its socialist goal? Neither socialism nor a planned economy have ever been built by a social-democratic government anywhere. There has been more nationalization by capitalist governments than by social-democratic ones, as in the Canadian experience. In the communist countries, everything was owned and controlled by the state, with a planned economy, but these countries failed to provide the people with a decent standard of living.

In recent years new challenges have confronted the NDP, such as keeping Canada together, protecting social legislation from being reduced and curtailed, and opposing the free trade agreement between Canada and the United States.

That agreement was merely a prelude to the inclusion of Mexico in the deal, broadening the agreement to include all of North America. The object of this arrangement is undoubtedly the de-industrialization of Ontario, Quebec, and the highly industrialized regions of the United States, in favour of the southern states and Mexico, where labour is much cheaper and largely unorganized. This is following a pattern which has been pursued for the last thirty years, in which Japan and the United States have been utilizing the poorer countries of Asia for cheap labour. The result of this policy is increased unemployment in the northern states of America, the vast growth of a homeless population, the decay of the big cities, the spectacular rise in crime, the failure to care for the sick and elderly, and the sky-rocketing debts of the federal, state, and municipal governments. In Canada, 400,000 jobs have been lost as a result of big and little corporations shutting down here and opening in Mexico and the southern states.

In an essay in the *New Yorker*, January 23, 1989, Robert Heilbroner, the well-known American economist, sang the praises of capitalism:

> Less than seventy-five years after it officially began, the contest between capitalism and socialism is over: capitalism has won.[15]

One can understand what Heilbroner means by capitalism, but his reference to "socialism," meaning the economies of the former Soviet bloc, is misleading. In a 1964 pamphlet, E. Varga, at that time the leading Soviet economist, concluded with this declaration:

> The twentieth century will go down in history as the century of the death of capitalism and the triumph of communism.[16]

In calling the Soviet system "communism," Varga differentiated its economy from any other. It would have been more appropriate for Heilbroner to say that the "contest between *capitalism* and *communism* is over, and capitalism has won."

Heilbroner's use of the term "capitalism" applies to the advanced industrial countries, which have solved the problem of distributing food, clothing, and consumer goods, as well as supplying raw materials and a labour force to produce more than enough to sell in the domestic and export markets. But capitalism has not solved the problems of the people who have become surplus to the labour market, and live in abject poverty. Nor does he say much about the Third World, which the advanced capitalist countries have systematically plundered and exploited, and where millions suffer starvation and disease.

All this underlines the need for and role of social democrats, in parliamentary parties and in mass movements, and explains why the NDP has become a significant public force. The surprise election of a NDP government in Ontario, followed by the election of NDP governments in British Columbia and Saskatchewan, indicate that the public approval of this party has grown.

Why then does the new wave of criticism by supporters and members of the NDP propose that the NDP discard many of its long-held principles and turn to the right? They argue, in part, from the collapse of the Soviet Union and the Eastern bloc, asserting that this has not only discredited Marxism, but the whole idea of socialism.

Bob Rae used the argument about the Soviet economy to explain why he is against the CCF-NDP concept of a planned economy, as quoted earlier:

> Yet socialists have to come to terms with some critical realities as well. The command economies of the East have been a disaster. "Planning" on its own does not work: it ignores too many choices, too many unknowns, too many actors in the system. It lacks dynamism, energy, a

> willingness to change: the key is to match our commitment
> to democracy, our commitment to security, our commit-
> ment to solidarity, with what we all must recognize as the
> positive aspect of markets.[17]

He then declares that "socialism must be seen as embracing a creative tension between three realities: planning, democracy, and markets." But the only experience with a planned economy in peace-time was the Soviet Union, which cannot be used as an argument to justify the CCF-NDP dropping its call for a planned economy.

The propaganda against the NDP has been mounting since the election of a NDP government in Ontario. From the day that this government took over it has been subjected to the most massive attacks ever directed at a party in power. And yet this is but a foretaste of how the opposition will attempt to discredit and undermine the NDP governments before the next election.

The opposition represents the biggest corporations in Canada, who are determined to oust this government at all cost. Any thought that they can be appeased by curtailing the NDP's program would be a mistake. The economy is in a recession, and the province of Ontario is the hardest hit in the country. The NDP government has already been compelled to drop some of its cherished projects, and will undoubtedly drop others, at least temporarily.

Social democracy as a political idea, standing in opposition to the liberal and conservative ideologies, has appeared in Canada from the turn of the century as the alternative to these policies. As such it appealed to sections of the farm and labour movements, and later to sections of the middle class, including teachers, social workers and academics. It never had much appeal to small business people. It became a more effective part of Canadian politics when it appeared as a political party, first as the Co-operative Commonwealth Federa-tion (CCF), then as the New Democratic Party (NDP) contesting for political power against the other parties. At first its main support was in the West, later it became firmly entrenched in Ontario, federally and provincially.

The evolution of social democracy in Canada has reflected the changes in the economic and political environment, domestically and on a world scale. These eventually found their way in changes of policy or in emphasis. But today Canadian social democracy faces its biggest challenges yet: to find a more realistic definition of socialism; to respond to the consequences of the de-industrialization of Canada

that the free trade agreement is bringing about; and to provide leadership to keep Canada together, on the basis of recognizing Quebec's
right to self-determination, and extending those rights to the aboriginal peoples.

Notes

One

1. James Mill, *An Essay on Government* (New York: Liberal Arts Press, 1965) 90.
2. Jeremy Bentham, *Works*, ed. Bowring (New York: 1962) 3: 311.
3. Frederick Engels, "The Condition of the Working Class in England," *On Britain* (Moscow: Foreign Languages Publishing House, 1962) 203.
4. Robert Owen, *A New View of Society* (New York: Everyman's Library, 1966) 54.
5. Owen, 17.
6. Owen, 86.
7. Owen, 149.
8. Frederick Engels and Karl Marx, *Correspondence, 1846–1895* (New York: International Publishers, 1935) 115–16.
9. Owen, 14.
10. Frederick Engels, *Ludwig Fuerbach* (New York: International Publishers, 1935) 74.
11. Owen, 262.
12. John Gray, *A Lecture on Human Happiness* (London: Sherwood Jones and Co., 1825) 52.
13. Gray, 15.
14. Gray, 34.
15. Marx and Engels, *On Britain* 361.
16. Marx and Engels, *On Britain* 494.
17. Marshall Cohen, ed., *The Philosophy of John Stuart Mill* (New York: The Modern Library, 1961) 42-43.
18. Cohen, 410.
19. John Stuart Mill, *Essays on Economics and Society* (Toronto: University of Toronto Press) 5: 713.
20. J. S. Mill, 750.
21. Cohen, 239–40.
22. Margaret Cole, *The Story of Fabian Socialism* (New York: Wiley and Sons, 1960) 28.

23. George Bernard Shaw, ed., *The Fabian Essays on Socialism* (Boston: publisher, date unknown) 36.
24. Shaw, 16.
25. Karl Marx, *The Civil War in France* (London: publisher unknown, 1933) 43.
26. Marx, *Civil War* 37.
27. Ramsay MacDonald, *Socialism and Society* (London: Independent Labour Party, 1905) 79.
28. MacDonald, 121.
29. Sidney Webb, *Socialism in England,* (New York: Scribner and Sons, 1893) 85.
30. Webb, 101.
31. Webb, 100.
32. Webb, 105.
33. Webb, 110–13.
34. Webb, 114–15.
35. Shaw, 12–13.
36. Shaw, 12–13
37. Engels, *Fuerbach* 272–73.
38. Arnold Toynbee, *The Industrial Revolution in Britain,* 1.
39. Oscar D. Skelton, *Socialism a Critical Analysis* (Boston: Houghton-Mifflin, 1911) 1.
40. Skelton, 2–3.
41. Skelton, 13–14.
42. Frederick Engels, *Condition of the Working Class* 277.

Two

1. Edward Porritt, *The Revolt in Canada Against the New Feudalism* (London: Cassell and Company, 1911).
2. After the execution of Louis Riel in 1885, the premier of Quebec, Honore Mercier, designated his Liberal Party as the National Party, which reverted to Liberal in 1896.
3. Henry George, *Progress and Poverty* (New York: Modern Library. First published 1879).
4. Gustavus Myers, *History of Canadian Wealth* (Chicago: Charles H. Kerr Publishers, 1914).
5. Porritt, *The Revolt in Canada Against The New Feudalism.*
6. J. A. Hobson, *Canada To-Day* (London: T. Fisher Unwin, 1906).
7. W. L. Morton, *The Progressive Party in Canada* (Toronto: University of Toronto Press, 1967).
8. At the same time, Upton Sinclair was writing his novel, *The Jungle,* about the Chicago stockyards, which was to create a sensation when it appeared in 1904.
9. Skelton, *Socialism, A Critical Analysis.*

10. O. D. Skelton, *General Economic History, 1896–1912* (Toronto: The Publishers Association of Canada, 1913) 273.

11. *The Grain Growers' Guide*, 25 June 1913.

12. Paul Sharp, *Agrarian Revolt in Western Canada* (New York: Octagon Books, 1971) 43.

13. E. C. Drury, "Canada and the Empire," *The Grain Growers' Guide*, 19 February 1913, 8.

14. *The Grain Growers' Guide*, 5 August 1914.

15. *The Grain Growers' Guide*, 12 August 1914.

16. Martin Robin, *Radical Politics and Canadian Labour 1880–1930* (Kingston: Industrial Relations Centre, 1968) 131–32.

17. Louis Aubrey Wood, *A History of Farmers' Movements in Canada*, 281–82.

18. Frederick J. Dixon, MPP, "Direct Legislation," *The Grain Growers' Guide*, 24 March 1915.

19. Robert Craig Brown and Ramsay Cook, *Canada 1896–1921* (Toronto: McClelland & Stewart Publishers, 1974) 319.

20. This was the prediction of *The Nation*, in an article of September 21, 1921 by A. Vernon Thomas.

21. Morton, *The Progressive Party in Canada*, 302–05.

22. *Manitoba Free Press*, 2 December 1921.

23. Murray Donnelly, *Dafoe of the Free Press* (Toronto: Macmillan, 1968) 106.

24. William Irvine, *The Farmers in Politics* (Toronto: McClelland & Stewart, 1920, 1976).

25. W. L. Mackenzie King, *Industry and Humanity* (Toronto: Macmillan, 1947) 179–80.

26. J. S. Woodsworth, "Organizing Democracy in Canada," *Western Labor News* Winnipeg, 23 August 1918.

27. J. S. Woodsworth, "What Next?" *Western Labor News*, 25 July 1919.

28. Woodsworth, "What Next?"

29. J. S. Woodsworth "What Next IV." *Western Labor News*, 15 August 1919.

30. See Norman Penner, *The Canadian Left* (Scarborough, Ont.: Prentice-Hall, 1977) 40–76, 171–217.

31. See Charles M. Johnston, *E. C. Drury, Agrarian Idealist* (Toronto: University of Toronto Press, 1986).

32. "The Resistance to 'Broadening Out,'" editorial, *Manitoba Free Press*, 15 December 1922.

33. See Paul Sharp, *Agrarian Revolt in Western Canada*, 141.

34. Alexander Franklin, "The Farmers Political Movement," *The Country Guide*, 15 October 1928, 33.

35. Kenneth McNaught, *A Prophet in Politics* (Toronto: University of Toronto Press, 1963) 215–20; Bruce Hutchison, *The Incredible Canadian* (Toronto: Longmans, Green and Company, 1953) 98–138.

36. Hutchison, 113.
37. On taking office in Quebec in 1937, Premier Maurice Duplessis signed the Act, ten years after it was passed in the House. Duplessis asked for $25,000,000 by way of compensation for the years the old people of Quebec had to do without it, but King refused.
38. Gad Horowitz, *Canadian Labour in Politics* (Toronto: University of Toronto Press, 1968) 30.

Three

1. The Labour Representation Association came into existence in 1901 and in 1906 it changed into the British Labour Party, a federated political party.
2. William M. Dick, *Labor & Socialism in America* (New York: Kennikat Press Port Washington, 1972) 29.
3. R. T. McKenzie, *British Political Parties* (New York and London: Frederick A. Praeger Publisher, 1963) 391.
4. Charles Lipton, *The Trade Union Movement in Canada 1827-1959* (Montreal: Canadian Social Publications Ltd., 1966) 82.
5. H. A. Logan, *Trade Unions in Canada* (Toronto: Macmillan, 1948) 18, 19, graph opposite 82.
6. *Trades and Labor Congress of Canada* (Report of Proceedings, 1917) 43–44.
7. See J. M. Beck, *Pendulum of Power* (Scarborough, Ont.: Prentice-Hall, 1968) 148. In *Radical Politics and Canadian Labour* Martin Robin states that there were 27 Labour candidates in English Canada, 136.
8. See Penner, *The Canadian Left* 63–64.
9. R. M. MacIver, *Labor in a Changing World* (Toronto: J. M. Dent, 1919) ix.
10. MacIver, 28.
11. See Penner, *Canadian Left* 177.
12. Richard Allen, *The Social Passion* (Toronto: University of Toronto Press, 1971).
13. Michiel Horn, *The League for Social Reconstruction* (Toronto: University of Toronto Press, 1980).
14. See Norman Penner, *Canadian Communism, The Stalin Years and Beyond* (Toronto: Methuen, 1988) 44–69.
15. Woodsworth, "Organizing Democracy."
16. J. S. Woodsworth, "Organizing Democracy in Canada," *Western Labor News* 25 July 1919.
17. J. S. Woodsworth, "The Labour Movement in the West," *The Canadian Forum* (April 1922): 587.
18. A. A. Heaps was elected to the House of Commons from North Winnipeg in 1925, defeating the incumbent E. J. McMurray. In his biography of his father, *The Rebel in the House* (London: Niccolo Publishing Company, 1970), Leo Heaps writes about this campaign, "The election

struggle in North Winnipeg had a sense of poetic justice about it. E. J. McMurray (a former Minister of Meighen's Cabinet and prominent Winnipeg lawyer) was one of the team of Crown Prosecutors at the strike trial." This is incorrect. McMurray was one of the defense lawyers at the strike trial, and Solicitor-General in Mackenzie King's Cabinet, not Meighen's. He became one of the outstanding defenders of civil rights in Canada.

19. Trades and Labor Congress of Canada, *Report of Proceedings*, 1928, 19.
20. John A. Cooper, B.A., LL.B., "Canadian Democracy and Socialism," *The Canadian Magazine* 3.4 (August, 1894): 332–36.
21. See McNaught, 157–230; and Penner, *Canadian Left*, 171–217.
22. House of Commons Debates, 10 April 1922, 829–44
23. Hutchison, 78.
24. J. S. Woodsworth, "A Labor Minority in the Canadian Parliament," *The Socialism of Our Times*, ed. Harry Lardler and Norman Thomas, (New York: Vanguard Press, 1929) 135.
25. See McNaught, 212.
26. Mackenzie King Papers, King to Hay 9 July 1923 quoted in Peter Oliver, *Public & Private Persons* (Toronto: Clarke, Irwin & Co., 1975) 133.
27. Charles M. Johnston, *E. C. Drury, Agrarian Idealist* (Toronto: University of Toronto Press, 1986) 88–89.
28. J. S. Woodsworth, House of Commons *Debates*, 9 March 1927, 1036-1043.

Four

1. Michiel Horn, *League*.
2. House of Commons *Debates*, 1 February 1933.
3. "Highlights From the Capital," *Winnipeg Free Press* 7 February 1933.
4. "Mr. King and the C.C.F.," *The Canadian Forum* April 1933: 243.
5. Hutchison, 183.
6. Mackenzie King, House of Commons *Debates*, 27 February 1933, 2500.
7. Ibid. 2497.
8. F. R. Scott, "The C.C.F. Convention," *The Canadian Forum* September, 1933: 448–49.
9. J. S. Woodsworth, letter to Mr. G. H. Williams, 6 March 1934, Saskatchewan Archives.
10. *Les Memoires d'Alfred Charpentier* (Quebec: Les Presses de l'Universite Laval, 1971) 163–64.
11. Charpentier, 164.
12. P. E. Trudeau, "Practice and Theory of Federalism," *Social Purpose for Canada*, ed. Michael Oliver (Toronto: University of Toronto Press, 1961) 375.
13. David E. Smith, *Prairie Liberalism*, (Toronto: University of Toronto Press, 1975) 199.

14. Quoted in Gerald L. Caplan, *The Dilemma of Canadian Socialism* (Toronto: McClelland and Stewart, 1973) 31.
15. William Irvine, M., House of Commons *Debates* 5 June 1922, 2502.
16. William Aberhart, letter to Mackenzie King, reprinted in Michiel Horn, *The Dirty Thirties* (Toronto: Copp Clark, 1972) 664.
17. Richard Wilbur, *H. H. Stevens 1878–1973* (Toronto: University of Toronto Press, 1977) 183.
18. Hutchison, 191.
19. Hutchison, 192.
20. Penner, *Canadian Communism* 110–11.
21. Penner, *Canadian Left* 147–56.
22. Michael Harrington, *Socialism* (New York: Saturday Review Press, 1970) 259–62.
23. Irving Abella, ed., *On Strike* (Toronto: James Lorimer & Company, Publishers, 1975).
24. Irving Abella, *Nationalism, Communism, and Canadian Labour* (Toronto: University of Toronto Press, 1973) 1–53.
25. Abella, *On Strike* 65–85; Penner, *Canadian Left* 188–90.
26. Alvin Finkel, *The Social Credit Phenomenon in Alberta* (Toronto: University of Toronto Press, 1989) 49–51.
27. J. S. Woodsworth, "The Question of A United Front," *The Commonwealth* 20 Mar. 1936.
28. David Lewis, "The CCF Convention," *The Canadian Forum* September 1936: 7.
29. Frank H. Underhill, "The CCF Takes Stock," *The Canadian Forum* August 1936: 10.
30. Scott, Marsh, Spry, Gordon, Forsey, Parkinson, *Social Planning for Canada*, (1935) 501–11; *Canada — One or Nine?*, (League for Social Reconstruction, 1938) 30–31.
31. Upton Sinclair, "Explaining Our Politics," *The Llano Colonist*, Louisiana, 22 August 1936.

Five

1. David Lewis, *The Good Fight* (Toronto: Macmillan, 1981) 165–89.
2. Lewis, *Good Fight* 170.
3. J. S. Woodsworth, House of Commons *Debates*, 8 September 1939, 47.
4. M. J. Coldwell (Rosetown-Biggar), House of Commons *Debates* 9 September 1939 55.
5. Cable from Arthur Greenwood, acting leader of the British Labour Party at *Emergency National Council Meeting*, House of Commons, Ottawa, 6, 7, 8 September 1939, 4 and 5.
6. Lewis, *Good Fight* 177–78.
7. Heaps, *Rebel* 161.
8. M. J. Coldwell, letter, 10 September 1941, National Archives MG28 IV 1, Volume 91, under "Individuals." Also Norman Penner, "They Fought

for Labor — Now Interned!" which is the report of the delegation of families of people who had been interned for their activity in or around the Communist Party.

9. MG28 IV 1 Vol. 2 National Executive Meeting March 21–22, 1941.
10. David Lewis and Frank Scott, *Make This Your Canada*, (Toronto: Canada Control Publishing, 1943) 208–13.
11. See Abella, *Nationalism*, and Horowitz, *Canadian Labour*.
12. From Minutes of National Executive Meeting, 19–20 September 1942: 2.
13. Abella, *Nationalism* 75.
14. Penner, *Canadian Communism* 189.
15. Caplan, *Dilemma* 105.
16. March 1943, Ontario Archives, Queen's University.
17. E. B. Jolliffe, letter to Nelson Alles, MPP, William Riggs MPP, and George Bennett MPP, 26 September 1944, Queen's University Archives.
18. David Lewis, letter to Angus H. McDonell, 4 November 1943, NAC CCF Papers MG28 IV Vol. 13 — Convention Correspondence.
19. Mackenzie King Diaries, 6 December 1942 in *The Mackenzie King Record*, J. W. Pickersgill, ed. (Toronto: U of T Press, 1960) vol. 1: 434.
20. Lewis and Scott, *Make This Your Canada* 24.
21. Lewis and Scott, 84.
22. Lewis and Scott, 177.
23. Lewis and Scott, 164.
24. *Planning for Freedom*, A Presentation of CCF Principles, Policy, & Program, Ottawa, December 1944.
25. M. J. Coldwell, *Left Turn, Canada* (London: Victor Gollancz Ltd., 1945).
26. Lewis, 293.

Six

1. F. R. Scott, *Opening Address of the National Chairman*, July, 1950, ("Report Eleventh National Convention, Co-operative Commonwealth Federation") NAC, MG 28 IV 1, Vol. 18.
2. Scott, *Opening Address*.
3. Scott, *Opening Address*.
4. See Horowitz, Chapter 3 "The Struggle with the Communists, 1943–48" 85–131; Abella, *Nationalism* 213–22.
5. R. H. S. Crossman, M. *Address to the Fourteenth National Convention of the CCF*, Winnipeg, 1 August 1956, 3 NAC MG IV 1, Vol. 20. Also quoted in Lewis, *Good Fight* 448.
6. National Convention Reports as above, 1956, 19.
7. Tariq Ali, ed., *The Stalinist Legacy* (London: Penguin Books, 1984) Secret Report by Nikita S. Khrushchev to the 20th Congress of the Communist Party of the Soviet Union, 221–72.
8. Lewis, *Good Fight* 441.

9. Stanley Knowles, letter to Harold Winch, 18 August 1957, CCF Archives, MG28 IV 1 Vol. 90.

10. Extract from Proceedings of the Second Biennial Convention of the Canadian Labour Congress, April 1958, quoted in Jack Williams, *The Story of Unions in Canada*, (Toronto: J. M. Dent and Sons Ltd., 1975) 219.

11. Susan Mann Trofimenkoff, *Stanley Knowles* (Saskatoon: Western Producer Prairie Books, 1982) 161.

12. Desmond Morton, *NDP The Dream of Power* (Toronto: Hakert, 1974) 28.

13. Frank Feigert, *Canada Votes 1935–1988* (Durham, N.C.: Duke University Press, 1991).

14. Canadian Parliamentary Guide 1989, 242–367.

15. James Laxer, *Rethinking the Economy* (Toronto: NC Publications, 1984) 1–8.

16. CCF-NDP Papers in the Public Archives of Canada, MG IV 28 Volume 366 Book 3 20 November 1964.

17. PAC, Ottawa CCF-NDP Papers MG 28 IV Volume 366 Book 4 17–19 June 1966. In his book *NDP The Dream of Power*, 91, Desmond Morton describes a weekend conference with David Lewis, Charles Taylor, and Kari Levitt in December 1968 on this same subject.

18. Kari Levitt, *Silent Surrender — The Multinational Corporation in Canada* (Toronto: Macmillan of Canada, 1970).

19. Leon Dion, *Nationalismes et politiques au Québec* 100.

20. Statement by T. C. Douglas, 16 February 1968, PAC MG 28 IV Vol. 367, Book 6.

21. NDP Federal Council Meeting, Winnipeg, March 1–3, 1968 MG28 IV Vol. 367, Book 6.

22. Doris French Shackleton, *Tommy Douglas* (Toronto: McClelland & Stewart, 1975) 286; Thomas and Ian McLeod, *Tommy Douglas* (Edmonton: Hurtig, 1987) 268; Desmond Morton, *The New Democrats 1961–1986* (Toronto: Copp, Clark, Pitman, 1986) 86.

23. Tommy Douglas, letter to Mr. C. A. Scotton, 6 May 1969.

24. *The New Democrat*, Sept.–Oct. 1969, 6–7.

Seven

1. Trudeau, 375.

2. The Right Honourable, the Prime Minister of Canada, Pierre Elliot Trudeau, a Canadian Government News Release, delivered on television, Thursday, 2 October 1980.

3. The Right Honourable Pierre Elliot Trudeau was given an honorary degree in Law at the University of Toronto, 14 March 1991. In his address, he launched into a strong attack on the judgement of the Supreme Court of 28 September 1981, and blamed it for whatever weaknesses the Charter of Rights has displayed since then.

4. House of Commons *Debates*, 30 November 1981, 13497.
5. *Excerpts from the Quebec NDP Program*, National Archives MG 28 IV 1, Volume 424 Federal Election 1972.
6. Ibid.
7. Andre Lamoureux, *le NPD et le Québec 1958–1985* (Montreal: Editions du Parc, 1985) 153.
8. *Montreal Gazette*, 15 February 1990.

Eight

1. Frank Scott, in Walter Young, *The Anatomy of a Party, The National CCF* (Toronto: University of Toronto Press, 1969) 111.
2. McLeod and Mcleod, 139.
3. T. C. Douglas Papers, Saskatchewan Archives Board File 413 R331 Marked #308 "A Four-Year Plan" 29 November 1947 2.
4. "A Four-Year Plan."
5. "A Four-Year Plan," 2.
6. "A Four-Year Plan," 18.
7. Shackleton, 164–65.
8. Finkel, 73.
9. McLeod and McLeod, 108.
10. From *Report of Saskatchewan Health Services Survey Commission, 1944* quoted in McLeod and McLeod, 147.
11. McLeod and McLeod, 194.
12. C. H. Higginbotham, *Off the Record: The CCF in Saskatchewan* (Toronto: McClelland and Stewart, 1968) 87.
13. McLeod and McLeod, 203.
14. See Shackleton, 286, and McLeod and McLeod, 268.
15. Evelyn Eager, *Saskatchewan Government, Politics and Pragmatism* (Saskatoon: Western Producer Prairie Books, 1980) 186–87.
16. R.E.O.R.T. from RCMP Files, 9 June 1919, a description of a speech made by J. S. Woodsworth, which the RCMP calls "Bolshevism at Winnipeg."
17. Ramsay Cook, *The Politics of John W. Dafoe and the Free Press* (Toronto: University of Toronto Press, 1963) 122–23.
18. See Nelson Wiseman, *Social Democracy in Manitoba, A History of the CCF-NDP* (Winnipeg: The University of Manitoba Press, 1983) 10–23.
19. Wiseman, 24–36.
20. From an interview given by Edward Schreyer to Jean-Marc Hebert, in Winnipeg, 18 May 1990.
21. See Wiseman, 125–46.
22. Supreme Court of Canada, *In the Matter of, Section 55 of the Supreme Court Act*, R.S.C. 1970 c.S-19, as amended; Judgement rendered, 13 June 1985. 27.
23. *A Message from Manitoba Grassroots to the People of Manitoba* an advertisement in the *Winnipeg Sun*, 23 June 1985.

24. Howard Pawley, interview in Winnipeg, 16 July 1990, by Jean-Marc Hebert.
25. See Martin Robin, *British Columbia in Canadian Provincial Politics* 2nd ed. (Scarborough, Ont.: Prentice-Hall, 1978) 28–60.
26. See Martin Robin, *The Rush for Spoils* (Toronto: McClelland and Stewart, 1972) and *Pillars of Profit*.
27. Quote in Allan Fotheringham's column in *B.C. — Politics and Government*, 24 May 1974: 35.
28. Fotheringham.
29. Lorne J. Kavic and Garry Brian Nixon, *The 1200 Days — A Shattered Dream* (Coquitlam, B.C.: Kaen Publishers, 1978).
30. Philip Resnick, *Social Democracy in Power, The Case of British Columbia*, (Vancouver: B.C. Studies, 1977).
31. Christopher Harris, *The NDP Government, A Failure of Co-ordination and Political Judgement*, M.A. Thesis, University of British Columbia, 4.
32. Interview by William King with Ken Rivkin, 18 May 1990.
33. The Vancouver *Province* 10 October 1973.
34. Jack Munro and Jane O'Hara, *Union Jack: Labour Leader Jack Munro* (Vancouver: Douglas & McIntyre, 1988) 82.
35. In *B.C. Politics and Policy*, March 1990: 2.
36. Donald C. MacDonald, *The Happy Warrior* (Toronto: Fitzhenry and Whiteside, 1988) 396.
37. House of Commons *Debates*, February 1, 1933.

Nine

1. Woodsworth, "What Next?" 25 July 1919.
2. Bob Rae, "What We Owe Each Other", Speech to the University of Waterloo, 10 Jan. 1990: 3–4.
3. Rae, 5.
4. Rae, 17.
5. John Richards, Robert D. Cairns, and Larry Pratt, eds., *Social Democracy Without Illusions* (Toronto: McClelland & Stewart 1991); Simon Rosenblum and Peter Findlay, eds. *Debating Canada's Future* (Toronto: James Lorimer & Company, 1991).
6. Richards et al., 50.
7. Richards et al., 58.
8. Richards et al., 59.
9. Richards et al., 61.
10. Richards et al., 191–200.
11. Rosenblum and Findlay, 11–28.
12. John A. Cooper, "Canadian Democracy and Socialism," *Canadian Magazine* 3.4 (August 1894): 335.
13. See Penner, *The Canadian Left*, 200–202.

14. Terry Morley, "Canada and the Romantic Left," *Queen's Quarterly*, 86.1 (Spring 1979): 110–19.
15. Robert Heilbroner, "The Triumph of Capitalism," *The New Yorker* 23 Jan. 1989: 98.
16. E. Varga, *Twentieth Century Capitalism*, (Moscow: Progress Publishers, 1964).
17. Bob Rae, 35.

Selected Bibliography

Allen, Richard. *The Social Passion*. Toronto: University of Toronto Press, 1971.

Archer, Keith. *Political Choices and Electoral Consequences*. Montreal-Kingston: McGill-Queens University Press, 1990.

Avakumovic, Ivan. *Socialism in Canada*. Toronto: McClelland & Stewart, 1978.

Baron, Don and Jackson, Paul. *Battleground: The Socialist Assault on Grant Devine's Canadian Dream*. Toronto: Bedford Publishing, 1991.

Bealey, Frank and Pelling, Henry. *Labour and Politics* 1900–1906, London: Macmillan, 1958.

Berton, Pierre. *The Great Depression*. Toronto: McClelland & Stewart, 1990.

Bland, Salem. *The New Christianity*. Toronto: University of Toronto Press, 1973.

Brennan, J. William (Editor). *Building the Cooperative Commonwealth*. Regina: Canadian Plains Reasearch Centre, 1985.

Bronner, Stephen Eric. *Socialism Unbound*. New York: Routledge, 1990.

Caplan, Gerald L. *The Dilemma of Canadian Socialism*. Toronto: McClelland & Stewart, 1973.

Cole, G. D. H. and Postgate, Raymond. *The Common People*. London: Methuen, 1966.

Conway, J. F. *The West*. Toronto: James Lorimer & Company, 1983.

Cook, Ramsay. *The Regenerators*. Toronto: University of Toronto Press, 1985.

—*The Politics of John W. Dafoe and the Free Press*. Toronto: University of Toronto Press, 1963.

Crowley, Terry, *Agnes MacPhail and the Politics of Equality*. Toronto: James Lorimer Publishers, 1990.

Dwja, Sandra. *The Politics of the Imagination: A Life of F.R. Scott*. Toronto: McClelland & Stewart, 1987.

Elliot, David R. and Miller, Iris. *Bible Bill*. Edmonton: Reidmore Books, 1987.

Feigert, Frank. *Canada Votes 1935-1988*. Durham: Duke University Press, 1989.

Finkel, Alvin. *The Social Credit Phenomenon in Alberta*. Toronto: University of Toronto Press, 1989.

—*Business and Social Reform in the Thirties*. Toronto: James Lorimer & Company, 1979.

George, Henry. *Progress and Poverty*. New York: The Modern Library, no date.

Good, W. C. *Is Democracy Doomed?* Toronto: The Ryerson Press, 1933.

Harrington, Michael. *Socialism*. New York: Saturday Review Press, 1970.

—*Socialism Past and Future*. New York: Arcade Publishing, 1989.

—*Toward A Democratic Left*. New York: The Macmillan Company, 1968.

Heaps, Leo. *The Rebel in the House*. London: Niccolo Publishing Company, 1970; Toronto: Fitzhenry & Whiteside Limited, 1984.

—*Our Canada*. Toronto: James Lorimer & Company, 1991.

Hobson, John. *Canada To-day*. London: Fisher Unwin, 1906.

Howard, Victor. *"We Were the Salt of the Earth!"* Regina: Canadian Plains Research Centre, 1985.

Howe, Irving. *Socialism and America*. New York: Harcourt Brace Jovanovich, New York, 1985.

Innis, Harold, (Editor). *Labor in Canadian-United States Relations*. Toronto: The Ryerson Press, 1937.

Irvine, William. *The Farmers in Politics*. Toronto: McClelland & Stewart, 1920.

Irving, John. *The Social Credit Movement in Alberta*. Toronto: University of Toronto Press, 1968.

Jenson, Jane, and Brodie, Janine. *Crisis, Challenge, and Change*. Ottawa: Carleton University Press, 1988.

Johnston, Charles. *E. C. Drury*. Toronto: University of Toronto Press, 1986.

Lamoureux, Andre. *le NPD et le Quebec 1958-1985*. Montreal: Editions du Parc, 1985.

Laurie, Bruce. *Artisans Into Workers*. New York: The Noonday Press, 1989.

Laxer, Robert and James. *The Liberal Idea of Canada*. Toronto: James Lorimer & Company, 1977.

Laycock, David. *Populism and Democratic Thought in the Canadian Prairies 1910-1945*. Toronto: University of Toronto Press, 1990.

Lerner, Warren. *A History of Socialism and Communism in Modern Times*. Englewood Cliffs, N.J.: Prentice-Hall Inc. 1982.

Levenstein, Harvey A. *Communism, Anti-Communism, and the CIO*. Westport, Conn.: Greenwood Press, 1981.

Levesque, Andree. *Virage a Gauche Interdit*. Montreal: Boreal Express, 1984.

Lewis, David. *The Good Fight*. Toronto: Macmillan of Canada, 1981.

Lipset, Seymour Martin. *Agrarian Socialism*. New York: Doubleday, 1968.

Lovett, William. *Life and Struggles of William Lovett*. London: Macgibbon, 1920.

MacDonald, Donald C. *The Happy Warrior*, Toronto: Fitzhenry & Whiteside, 1988.

MacIver, R. M. *Labor in the Changing World*. New York: J. M. Dent, 1919.

Macpherson, C. B. *Democracy in Alberta*. Toronto: University of Toronto Press, 1962.

Mardiros, Anthony. *William Irvine*. Toronto: McClelland & Stewart, 1979.

Marx, Karl and Engels, Frederick. *On Britain*. Moscow: Foreign Languages Publishing House, 1962.

McDonald, Lynn. *The Party that Changed Canada*. Toronto: Macmillan of Canada, 1987.

McLeod, Thomas and Ian. *Tommy Douglas*. Edmonton: Hurtig, 1987.

McNaught, Kenneth. *A Prophet in Politics*. Toronto: University of Toronto Press, 1959.

Mills, Allen. *Fool for Christ: The Political Thought of J. S. Woodsworth*, Toronto: University of Toronto Press, 1991.

Moore, Roger. *The Emergence of the Labour Party 1880-1924*. London: Hodder & Stoughton, 1978.

Morley, J. T. *Secular Socialists*. Montreal-Kingston: McGill-Queens University Press, 1984.

Morton, Desmond. *The New Democrats 1961-1986*. Toronto: Copp Clark Pitman, 1986.

Morton W. L. *Manitoba, A History*. Toronto: University of Toronto Press, 1957.

—*The Progressive Party in Canada*. Toronto: University of Toronto Press, 1967.

Munro, Jack and O'Hara, Jane. *Union Jack*. Vancouver: Douglas & McIntyre, 1988.

Myers, Gustavus. *History of Canadian Wealth*. Toronto: James Lorimer & Company, 1977.

Penner, Norman, (Editor). *Winnipeg 1919, The Strikers' Own History of the Winnipeg General Strike*. Toronto: James Lorimer & Company, 1973, 1975.

—*The Canadian Left*. A Critical Analysis, Scarborough, Ont.: Prentice-Hall, 1977.

—*Canadian Communism, The Stalin Years and Beyond*. Toronto: Methuen, 1988.

Pennington, Doris. *Agnes MacPhail*. Toronto: Simon & Pierre, 1989.

Porritt, Edward. *The Revolt in Canada Against the New Feudalism*. London: Cassell and Company, 1911.

Richards, John, Pratt, Larry, Cairns, Robert D.(Editors). *Social Democracy Without Illusions*. Toronto: McClelland & Stewart, 1991.

Robin, Martin. *Radical Politics and Canadian Labour*. Kingston: Industrial Relations Centre, 1968.

Rosenblum, Simon, Findlay, Peter. *Debating Canada's Future*. Toronto, James Lorimer & Company, 1991.

Shackleton, Doris French. *Tommy Douglas*. Toronto, McClelland & Stewart, 1975.

Sharp, Paul. *Agrarian Revolt in Western Canada*. New York: Octagon, 1971.

Shaw, Bernard. (Editor) *Fabian Essays*. London: George Allen, 1950.

Skelton, O. D. *Socialism, A Critical Analysis*. Cambridge: Houghton and Mifflin, 1911.

Smith, David E. *Prairie Liberalism*. Toronto: University of Toronto Press, 1975.

Smith, Cameron. *Unfinished Journey: The Lewis Family*. Toronto: Summerhill Press, 1989.

Smith, Douglas. *Joe Zuken*. Toronto: James Lorimer & Company, 1990.

Smith, Goldwin. *Canada and the Canadian Question*. Toronto: University of Toronto Press, 1971.

Stanley, George F. G. *The Birth of Western Canada*. Toronto: University of Toronto Press, 1970.

Stubbs, Lewis St. George. *A Majority of One*. Winnipeg: Queenston House, 1983.

Swerdlow, Max. Brother Max: *Labour Organizer and Educator*. St. John's: The Committee on Canadian Labour History, 1990.

Thompson, T. Phillips. *The Politics of Labor*. Toronto: University of Toronto Press, 1975.

Tracey, Herbert. *The Book of the Labour Party*. London: Caxton Publishing.

Trofimenkoff, Susan Mann. *Stanley Knowles*. Saskatoon: Western Producer Prairie Books, 1982.

Tyre Robert. *Douglas in Saskatchewan*. Vancouver: Mitchell Press, 1962.

Underhill, Frank. *In Search of Canadian Liberalism*. Toronto: Macmillan, 1960.

Valelly, Richard M. *Radicalism in the States*. Chicago: University of Chicago Press, 1989.

Wiseman, Nelson. *Social Democracy in Manitoba*. Winnipeg: The University of Manitoba, 1983.

Wood, Louis Aubrey. *A History of Farmers' Movement in Canada*. Toronto: University of Toronto Press, 1975.

Woodsworth, J. S. *My Neighbor*. Toronto: University of Toronto Press, 1972.

Young, Walter D. *The Anatomy of A Party: The National CCF, 1932-61*. Toronto University of Toronto Press, 1969.

Index

Aberhart, William, 61, 62-63
Action Libérale nationale (ALN), 58
All-Canadian Congress of Labour
    (ACCL), 46
Amalgamated Clothing Workers, 57
American Federation of Labor
    (AFL), 34, 38, 39, 67
American Labor Union, 39
American Socialist Labor Party, 18
Argue, Hazen, 94

Barrett, Dave, 129, 131
Bax, Belfort, 9
Bellamy, Edward, 47
Bennett, R. B., 54, 55, 63, 63-64
Bentham, Jeremy, 2
Beveridge Report, 80
Beveridge, William, 91
Bilingualism and Manitoba NDP,
    125-126
Blakeney, Allan, 120, 139
Bland, Salem, 30
Blatchford, Robert, 9
Bolshevik regime, support for in
    Canada, 42, 43
Bolsheviks, and socialism, 48
Booth, C. S., 75
Borden, Robert, 27
Bourassa, Robert, 110
Bracken, John, 84, 122
Breaugh, Michael, 96
Brewin, Andrew, 96
British Columbia, 59
British Columbia NDP,
    and anti-socialist coalition, 128-129
    and socialism, 129-130, 131, 132
    and the unions, 130-131

British immigrants, 1, 14, 32
British labour movement, 39
British Labour Party, 2, 11, 18
British North America Act (BNA
    Act), 1, 50-51, 55, 56, 88
British socialism, character of, 9-14
Broadbent, Ed, 96, 98, 102, 107,
    109, 124
    support for Ottawa, 121, 124
Buck, Tim, 65, 84

Calgary conference. *See* Co-opera-
    tive Commonwealth Federation
    (CCF), founding of
Canadian Congress of Labour
    (CCL), 67, 77, 94
Canadian Forum, 54, 56, 69
Canadian Labour Congress, merger
    with CCF, 89, 91-95
Canadian Labour Party, 32, 34, 44,
    45, 46
Canadian Tribune, 82
Capitalism, 144-145
Caplan, Gerald, 78
Cappon, Paul, 110
Catholic Church, and CCF, 58-59
Chamberlain, Neville, 74
Charter of Rights, 106
Chartist movement, 6, 16
Churchill, Winston, 75, 85
Clarke, William, 9
Cliche, Robert, 105
Coldwell, M. J., 68, 73, 74, 83, 84
Committee for Industrial Organiza-
    tion. *See* Congress of Industrial
    Organizatons